BRIAN'S JOURNEY

BRIAN'S JOURNEY

A Mother's Healing After
the Death of Her Son

Janet Dubrasky

LUMINARE PRESS
WWW.LUMINAREPRESS.COM

Brian's Journey
Copyright © 2020 by Janet Dubrasky

All rights reserved. This book or any portion thereof may not be reproduced or used in any manner whatsoever without the express written permission of the publisher, except for the use of brief quotations in a book review.

Printed in the United States of America

Cover Design by Melissa K. Thomas

Luminare Press
442 Charnelton St.
Eugene, OR 97401
www.luminarepress.com

LCCN: 2020910167
ISBN: 978-1-64388-364-9

I wish to dedicate this book to my husband, Jim, and my son, Michael, for their love and support. They are the reason I get up each day and put one foot in front of the other.

To all the parents who have lost a child, regardless of how they passed. Know that the souls of our loved ones are close by. Each time we think of them, their essences surround us with love. Know that we will unite with their souls when our journeys are complete, and know this: every day we are one day closer to that heavenly meeting.

Blessings!
jd

Table of Contents

Prologue 1

Chapter One
The Beginning, 1982–1985 3

Chapter Two
1986–1990 18

Chapter Three
1991–1995 26

Chapter Four
1996–1999 33

Chapter Five
2000–2005 42

Chapter Six
2006–2009 56

Chapter Seven
2010–2015 63

Chapter Eight
2016–2017 72

Chapter Nine
January–March 2018 115
Pictures 116–131

CHAPTER TEN
April–May 2018 169

CHAPTER ELEVEN
Reading with Tim Braun 178

CHAPTER TWELVE
June–November 2018 181
Reading with Kirsten Ross 186

CHAPTER THIRTEEN
December 2018 193
Reading with Patrick Mathews 194–195

CHAPTER FOURTEEN
2019 196

CHAPTER FIFTEEN
Signs and Connections 201

CHAPTER SIXTEEN
Letter to Brian, 1985 203

CHAPTER SEVENTEEN
Life Changes and Thank-Yous 205

Acknowledgements 211

Prologue

Where does a mother start with losing a child? How can I begin to explain the horrific grief? One instant he is here, and the next he is gone from this earth to another plane, the other side, or *heaven* as us mortals call it. I have to believe he is in heaven with his grandparents; his cousin, Jesse; aunts and uncle; and his best friends, Tommy and Drew.

I remember every detail of that day. How will I ever forget? It still pains me and always will. A mother never forgets. The love in my heart for my firstborn goes beyond death, even though I know he passed through me when he left this world to the next. I knew he passed before it was confirmed it was my Brian who jumped to his death on that beautiful winter morning in San Diego on Thursday, February 15, 2018 at 9:30 a.m.

Chapter One

The Beginning, 1982–1985

J im and I met in 1982, and we both felt such an attraction. He was thirty-two, and I was twenty-seven. After being single for all those years, I finally found the love of my life. We were married on January 8, 1983. For both of us, it was a dream come true, finding our soul mate. In early March of 1983, I miscarried, and even though we were devastated, we knew we would have children when the time was right. The doctor recommended I get pregnant in three months or so after giving my body a rest.

True to the doctor, I got pregnant in June and was due March 3, 1984. After fifteen hours of back labor—and our baby being three weeks late (more on that later in the book)—the baby was in distress, and so was I. My blood pressure was sky-high; and Dr. Edwards, watching the monitor, could see the baby's heart rate was going down. Dr. Edwards made the decision quickly to do a cesarean section.

Jim was with me the whole time and reported that our baby boy had the cord around his neck and had done a bowel movement while in distress. Our baby was cleaned up, and Jim let me know he had ten fingers and ten toes.

He was seven pounds, twenty ounces, and twenty and one-quarter inches long. We named him Brian Anthony. I was elated to have my baby healthy. I could not wait to hold him and breastfeed him. The love that poured out of me to this newborn was unimaginable. My mother told me it would be magic—and was she ever right. The instant I held him, I fell in love with this gift that God gave me to love, protect, and raise. At a time earlier in my life, I truly thought I would never want to have children, especially being from a large family. My mom said something so profound: "Then you will have none to make you laugh and none to make you cry."

He took to my breast like a duck to water. He was just perfect, a cherub; he was so beautiful that all the nurses in the nursery held him. When he cried, it was loud, because he wanted his mommy, not a fake breast—he wanted me. I was sore from the surgery and had complications from the anesthetic, so the nurses let me rest. God bless those wonderful nurses at Santa Monica Hospital; they were the best. When he was brought to me, he immediately relaxed, knowing it was his mommy. I was his world, and he was mine while we were alone in that room. When his pediatrician came in and I said, "Hi," he looked up; and she said to me, "He knows your voice." I wanted to say, "Of course he does; he's been inside me for almost ten months." Instead, I looked at my baby and was so proud of him—and knew he was special because he was mine and Jim's, created with love.

When we got home after seven days in the hospital, we were a family. We now had this little baby to take care of on our own. We were so careful to keep our hands washed and everything clean for our little Brian. He was so adorable and so angelic. I could not stop looking at him with total amazement that he was ours. I had no problem getting up with him for night feedings; it was such a pleasure, just he and I. I managed to sleep when he did and loved being a mommy for the first time.

My mom flew in on March 26th to see her fourth grandchild. Jim picked her up at Los Angeles International Airport (LAX), and as soon as she came in the door, after hugging me, she picked up Brian and said, "You've been here before, little man." She was a great help for three days so I could rest. She loved bathing him and just being Nana to her fourth grandchild. After three days—my mother always said—"You start to smell like fish, so time to go home." And that's what she did.

I promised to fly when I could bring Brian to see his Papa and cousin, Jesse. Brian's doctor agreed we could fly after he was four weeks old. I booked a flight to Las Vegas on April 17, 1984 for just Brian and me. He slept the whole way there. The flight attendants were very kind and kept coming over to see him; they all agreed he was "absolutely beautiful." We took a taxi to my mom's house, and there she was looking out her front window, waiting for us. She could not wait to see her new grandson again.

She was amazed at how much he had changed in several weeks. My dad and nephew, Jesse, who was five, were in awe at how perfect he was. My sisters Gail, Cathy, and Cindy were there to see Brian as well. The only ones missing were my sister Diane and my brother, Michael. I flew again with Brian in May to see Mom and Dad. We all sat down and selected a date to have our little man baptized, as I knew my mother wanted that for her grandchildren. Being raised Catholic, Jim and I thought it was important as well.

About six weeks after Brian was born, I decided it was time to start running again. I asked Jim if he could watch our little man while I went out for about thirty minutes. I was excited about getting some exercise again and enjoying the beautiful weather in early May. We were living in Playa Del Rey at the time, and I ran in the neighborhood and by the runways of LAX. As I was turning the corner of a street that was deserted and quite a distance from the houses, I noticed a black van. The van looked very ominous to me, and I had such a feeling that I needed to turn back right away. I had a terrible premonition that if I went by that van, I was in deep trouble. I turned back and went home. I dreamt that night that I would not have ever been seen again if I had run by that van. I prayed to God, thanking Him for saving me.

Sunday, June 3rd, we had Brian baptized, and we chose his godparents, Sal and Judy. It was a fabulous day; my mom flew in from Vegas, and of course Jim's parents were there and his grandmother Nonie. Brian seemed alert to all that was going on.

Mid-June, we moved to a house in the San Fernando Valley that Jim owned with a friend. We bought his friend out, and life began in our house. I started to notice that Brian was not a newborn anymore; he was smiling and laughing, standing up, and just into everything. I started giving him bottles. One morning, when he was only three months old, he could not wait for his bottle—to my surprise he grabbed it from my hands and put it in his mouth. I was shocked, as I remember thinking, "Wow, this is way too soon." After he went down for a nap, I called my mother, and she agreed three months was early.

One morning, I was changing Brian's diaper and was talking to him. My mouth was open, and he peed, a perfect shot in my mouth. Lesson number one: keep your mouth closed while changing a baby boy's diaper.

He started crawling and loved his walker. He was all over the place. No wonder I lost all my weight running after him. He started eating like there was no tomorrow. He loved his food and especially his juice bottle. My mom, having had six children, told me to give him cereal at night so he would sleep through the night. Did that ever work! I started making fresh foods for my little Brian: blending fresh broccoli, which he loved, and cube steak. It was fun, and he loved his food.

I got pregnant with our second child that summer when Brian was only four months old. When I told our pediatrician, she told me that was perfect. They would be close in age, and even though it would be hard in the beginning, I would be happy later on.

Brian continued to show us what a child learns and the different stages of growth. I loved taking him out to the store, park, car wash, or to his grandparents' house. (Jim's parents lived close by; mine were in Las Vegas.)

One day, I took him to the car wash. I will never forget holding him and watching the cars get washed. An elderly gentleman came up to me and said, "That is one beautiful baby." I of course said, "Thank you kindly." The man could not stop looking at Brian; he touched his head and said again, "How beautiful he is…" I can still see this man in my mind and will never forget the feeling of love and being so proud that Jim and I made such a beautiful son.

The following months were filled with visits to doctors' offices for Brian's shots and my ob-gyn visits.

My brother, Michael, had been diagnosed with cancer at the beginning of the year. With Michael being the only son, we were all devastated. My brother came for a visit as he wanted to go to San Diego and visit a Buddhist temple.

I remember his being so loving toward Brian and saying how fabulous he was. I look at the picture I took of them and can remember that day as if it were happening now. Michael stayed with us for a few days and then went on to see Mom and Dad in Las Vegas.

Brian started saying little things like "ma" and "da." His voice was so cute and sounded like an angel singing.

Brian loved the pool at his grandparents' house in North Hollywood. He loved water and was not afraid. I could not wait to see him every morning when he woke up. He would be standing in the crib with the biggest and brightest smile. After I changed him and got him his bottle, he would just look up at me. I would look at him with such wonder and awe! What an angel—so innocent and so pure. How could anyone hurt a baby or not want one. My heart filled with such love and tenderness.

That September my brother, Michael, went for another visit to see my parents and told us the news that his cancer had spread. He was given maybe a year or less. My heart was broken for my brother. He had never married and now would never have his own family. How could this be? My mom and dad were of course, heartbroken. Jim and I took Brian and stayed as long as we could. I am grateful for the family photo we had taken in my parents' yard that gorgeous September day.

Upon returning home after seeing my brother and family, our phone was ringing as we walked in the door. It was my mother and she said "Please don't be upset with me. Your dad wants to know if by any chance you took his teeth with you." I said, "What? His dentures? Mom, they are most likely where he put them." She said, "I know, sweetheart, but he cannot find them." Jim and I laughed so hard I thought we were going to bust a lung. My father is quite a character. Of course he found them—they were in his mouth!

As I continued to get bigger with my pregnancy and Brian was into everything, life became a routine. Jim would go to work at 7:00 a.m., and I would take care of Brian and make sure I laid down when he took a nap, as I was tired. Jim would get home around 5:30 or 6:00 p.m., and sometimes Brian would be fast asleep. Jim would be disappointed, so he would go to check on Brian and admire the creature we helped create.

Brian was a bundle of energy! He loved his toys and loved playing with other children. I went to Mommy and Me with him at various places I heard about. I had some friends with children that were Brian's age, and we had some lovely times comparing notes and watching the development of our precious children.

Brian started teething and his cheeks got so rosy. Of course, I called my mom as she always had the best home remedies for teething. She recommended a finger of brandy on his gums. At this time, at around six months, he was standing himself up on any chair or sofa. At seven months, he was not walking but running and falling, running and falling. By the end of the day, he was walking! Jim came home and was shocked. What happened to our little baby? The infant stage with Brian really did not last long. He seemed to be growing in front of our eyes.

Every day was full of new experiences for us and Brian. I was in a state of joy holding him and being with him. I was sad that Jim had to work and not see all the wonder of this little creature. He only had a few hours at night with him, if Brian was not already asleep when he got home from work, but definitely the weekends. I am grateful that I did not have to work and could be home taking care of him. My mother-in-law would watch him when I went to the doctor's office, and he would swim in the pool and loved being with his grandparents. But once I was there, he wanted mommy. I was delighted to be part of this little one's life and whole world at this time. In a few months, he would have a little sister or brother and it would not be just him anymore.

Thanksgiving was around the corner, and we went to Jim's parents' house with the promise we would visit my parents for Christmas. At this time, my brother was getting worse, and my mother had to go get him from Houston to Las Vegas. My sister, Gail, agreed to take care of him while my parents worked. My brother was not ready to die; he was only thirty-one years old. It broke my heart to see my only brother go through what he was going through. He was so young and had some much ahead of him. Why? Why was God doing this? I just did not understand.

Thanksgiving came and went, and it was December. On December 8th, Brian cut his first tooth. My poor baby had such a time with those teeth coming in. It was almost time for Christmas. Jim and I packed the car on December 21st with all the gifts for my parents and family. It was bittersweet seeing my brother lying on the sofa, as he could not walk anymore. His thirty-second birthday was the next day, December 22nd. He was happy to see us and held Brian in his arms. He was bald from all the chemo and radiation. The cancer was in his brain now, and you could see the lumps in the back of his head. I had to excuse myself and go cry upstairs. How my mom and dad held it together is beyond me.

My mother always made a lovely Christmas dinner and her famous trifle. Michael hardly ate, as he was so sick. He enjoyed just being with his family and knowing we all were there for him. He told us all how much he loved us. Jim and I drove back home a few days after Christmas and called to check on my brother. My dad told me it would not be long as Michael had gone into a coma. I arranged for my mother-in-law, Mimi, and Jim to take care of Brian, and I flew to Vegas. I was shocked to see my brother in a coma but still breathing. I let him know I was there, as they say the hearing is the last to go. My parent's anniversary was on that day, December 29th. I know my mom was hoping he would not pass on her and my dad's anniversary. Michael must have been aware because he left us at 3:00 a.m. on December 30th. I was up with him, and my hand was on his heart when it stopped. He had a fever. I kissed his forehead and told him it was OK to go, that we all loved him and he would be at peace with no more pain. My brother's death was the very first experience of true loss for me. Yes, my grandparents had all passed on, but seeing my sibling pass was gut wrenching. It was so traumatic and heartbreaking for me, and difficult to see my parents lose their only son.

We called 911, and an ambulance came. What was even harder was seeing your sibling put into a black bag covered all the way. Tears were streaming down my face, and I went to comfort my mom. The sun came up that morning, and I remember thinking, "How can this be? I just lost my only brother. How can life go on? How can the birds still sing and the world go on? Don't they know Michael is gone to heaven?"

I called Jim later that morning to ask if his mom would watch Brian for a few more days. Also, to see if he could fly to Vegas with a dress for me. I had not taken much when I left a few days earlier. Michael's wish was to be cremated. I helped my father make all the arrangements while my mother called family and friends to tell them. We had a viewing at the mortuary and then a beautiful mass the next day. Jim flew in, and we were going to fly back together after the mass and lunch. It was beautiful but so hard; here I was six months pregnant and very emotional. I also missed my Brian.

Before we left, I asked my mom how she was coping. She told me her faith and spirituality was helping her. She told me Michael was in heaven with Our Lord and would be there for us when it's our time.

We got home and immediately went to pick up Brian. I cannot believe how big he got in just four days! He put his arms out to me, and both of us immediately felt comforted. It's as if he knew mommy was sad and upset. He was smiling more, with his cute little grin. Brian gave me a reason to be grateful for life and the time my brother and I had growing up and supporting each other during our breaks-ups—his girlfriends and my boyfriends. One thing for sure, Michael loved Jim and told me I was very lucky to find him and have Brian.

New Year's Day came and went. Brian continued to amaze us with his growing and learning new things. He was teething pretty badly and started getting ear infections. We made lots of trips to his pediatrician, and he had to take medications. He was now walking and into everything. Brian loved the *Wizard of Oz* video, and I swear that he could recite the entire dialogue.

Brian's first birthday was lovely. We had a little party with cake and ice cream and family. Brian was too young to understand, but he sure loved the cake and ice cream. He was the life of the party, running here and there and visiting everybody and just being so darn cute!

April was coming fast and so would a new member of our family. We had to get Brian off the bottle at night and purchase him a new bed, since baby would need the crib. I spoke with Brian's pediatrician about how best to wean him off the bottle at night. She explained it would take three nights, and it would be hard for me to hear him cry, but if I did it as she said, it would be worth it. Yes, it broke my heart to hear my Brian cry at 2:00 a.m. for his bottle, but I went in there and told him, "No bottle tonight, sweetheart. You need to stop drinking a bottle as a new baby is coming." He cried for at least a half hour, and he finally fell asleep. The next night, it was the same thing, only this time it was maybe fifteen minutes, and on the third night only a few minutes. Amazing, yes!

We got his new bed. He liked sleeping in his big bed with rails. We kept talking to him about how a new baby was going to sleep in the crib and that he was going to be a big brother.

I was due with baby number two in early April. The doctor thought because I had a hard time with Brian, we should go ahead and plan another cesarean section for April 10th. Jim's mom would keep Brian, and Jim would go see Brian after work every day and stay with his mother and father as well. Jim was with me for the birth of our second son, Michael Christopher (of course named after my brother). Michael came into this world at 10:55 a.m. on Wednesday, April 10, 1985. He was eight pounds, eight ounces, and twenty-and-a-half inches long. Now we were a complete family, as neither of us wanted more children. Michael looked like a butterball; he was so cute and adorable and was chubby.

Jim came to get Michael and me five days after he was born. Jim's mom, Mary, would let us rest before she brought Brian home. I was not as tired with Michael or as sore, since I had not gone through the labor. I could not wait to see my little Brian after five days!

I was sitting in the den when Mary walked in with Brian. Michael was asleep in his crib. Brian looked at me and would not come to me. I was so shocked. He kept looking at me, and he would not let go of his grandma Mimi. I kept saying, "Brian, it's me, Mommy. Come here, sweetheart." He just stared at me and hung on to grandma. I then realized that I had changed since Michael was born, my big tummy that Brian would lay on was gone now. "Who is this woman who calls herself my mommy?" he must have thought. I sat down and asked Mary to go see Michael in his crib. That is when Brian came over to me and laid his head on my lap and cried. I picked him up and held him cooing to him that all was OK and that I was here for good.

I took him to meet his new brother. I carried him into the room he was now sharing with Michael. I told him this is your brother, Michael. Can you give the baby a kiss? Jim bent over with him and Brian gave his brother a kiss. It will forever be in my memory of that meeting of big brother and baby brother. It was just magical!

Adjusting to a one year old and a newborn was not easy at first. I was a little depressed, still grieving for my brother. It was hard juggling a baby and a toddler who was into everything. Those first few days were not easy, until the routine set in. I found Michael was a very hungry baby and that my breast was not enough for him. I had to supplement with a bottle. My mom came to help me after a week of being home, and even she could see how hard it was for me. She made a suggestion to give Michael a little cereal in his night feeding, as he was waking up every two hours. This poor soul was starved, and I just could not give him enough. My mother was right again. Michael slept longer and seemed more content on a full tummy.

Taking both boys to the pediatrician's office for their shots was no easy task. But I thought, if a mother can do it with twins, I can do it with a toddler and a newborn. Suffice it to say, I managed and found ways to enjoy the time with both boys. I would sing to them in the car and talk to them about what they were seeing on the way to the doctor's office.

I did look forward to the weekends when Jim was home to help me. We took turns sleeping in: his day to sleep in was Saturdays, and mine was Sundays. To this day, I still wake up early every day and manage to allow myself the comfort of sleeping in on Sundays.

Sadly, Jim's grandmother, Nonnie, passed away before Michael's baptism on Mother's Day, 1985. The following weekend, we had Michael baptized with Jim's brother, Andy, as godfather and his cousin Lucy as godmother. It was a wonderful celebration!

The weekends were busy with going to see both grandparents. Since mine were in Las Vegas, we would leave either late on Friday after work or very early on Saturday. If Jim were on vacation, we could stay with my parents a week or so, which my mother loved. Brian and Michael had their cousin, Jesse, who was five years older than Brian, that they loved being around.

In July of 1985, I was in the bathroom and all of a sudden I heard Brian scream. He came into the bathroom with blood dripping from his forehead. I could not imagine what happened; you cannot turn your back for a second. I picked him up and got a cloth to wipe his forehead and saw that he had a gash on his forehead that definitely needed stitches. He had run into the floor heater and fell, my poor baby. I did not panic and instead soothed him while holding him with the cloth.

Michael was asleep, and I held Brian while I called Jim and told him that I needed to take Brian to the emergency room right away. Jim's mom and dad were at least twenty minutes away. I then thought of our neighbor, Lillian across the street. I called her, and she came right over to look after Michael for me. I called Jim back and told him I would call after Brian was stitched up.

Nothing is harder than watching your baby get stitches in the emergency room. Brian was kicking and screaming, and I was helping hold him down and talking to him to be still and all would be OK. Granada Hills Hospital was so great and quickly stitched up my little Brian. Afterward, they gave him a red Popsicle, and he was a happy boy!

What an ordeal! The first is always the hardest, but you know all will be well.

When we got home, Lillian was feeding Michael and asked how Brian was. I thanked her profusely and asked if she ever needed anything to let me know. Having a neighbor like her was a godsend.

Life was busy that summer with not one but two growing babies. I tried to keep a schedule for them, but it was very hard to do with one running around all the time and into everything. Weekends were doing family things with the boys. For the most part, if we were not going to see my family or Jim's, we hung around the house and let Brian play outside. He loved being naked while I held Michael and Jim watched Brian. Brian loved holding something in his hands, a stick or anything he could hang onto. It was so much fun seeing him laugh and giggle whenever something funny happened. He loved being held by his daddy high up in the air.

At around five months, Michael decided he liked a cup instead of the bottle. Wow! How easy is that? Because Michael was a much bigger baby, he loved eating, and not just baby food. I had to feed him what we gave Brian. Both my babies loved food, and thank goodness neither had any food allergies.

One day in September, Mimi watched the boys so I could get my hair done. It was a treat to do this once in a while. I dropped them off, had my hair done, and went shopping a bit. I picked them up as promised, but it was getting dark outside and I forgot to leave the front light on. I was holding Michael in my arms and Brian by the hand trying to get the key in the lock. I was exasperated because I could not see and started to say "Son of a…" and Brian said, "bitch." I was totally shocked. It was funny coming out of an eighteen-month-old's mouth. I made a note to tell Jim to ask his father not to use language like that.

Brian learned very young how to negotiate. He did not like being told "no" and would ask the question in another way. If it were too early to go outside and play, he wanted to know "Why not?" and "How come?" He would say, "I will be quiet." If Jim was firm in saying "no," Brian would turn to him and say, "Mom's the boss." I was home with the boys, and Dad had to work. It was funny in a way that Brian and Michael knew that Mom was running the house and feeding them while Dad was home in the evenings and on weekends.

Chapter Two

1986–1990

Life became fun, watching the boys grow up and both having new experiences. Of course, the changes as parents are quite subtle, but other people notice. I loved waking up and walking into their room to see them. Brian was in his bed, and Michael would be fast asleep. I would change Brian and get him fed before Michael would wake up. Michael was a sleeper. He seemed to come into this world very hungry and tired. Brian came into this world ready to explore and kept busy every minute he could. Brian was talking in sentences now and loved always holding something in his hand.

We started to call Brian, "Mr. Rambunctious!" He was all over the place, and you could not take your eyes off him. He loved playing and getting into my pots and pans; he loved banging on the pots and pans with wooden spoons. It was pure joy seeing him exploring his world. Naturally, Michael followed suit in doing what his older brother was doing.

With Brian's second birthday approaching, and Michael's first, it was interesting seeing where we were in only two short years. Two children, only a year apart. Brian was still having a hard time with some of his teeth coming in, and

Michael had just gotten his first one. Brian had issues with ear infections and seemed to be on antibiotics all the time. His cheeks were forever rosy, and sometimes he would have fevers.

After so many ear infections, his pediatrician told us he needed eustachian tubes in his ears. We arranged for the surgery that spring. Jim took the day off for Michael, while I took Brian to the hospital for early morning surgery. We would be home later that day. After having gone through stitches with him, having them take my baby away for surgery was even more difficult. I wanted to go with him; he was screaming for his mama with his hands out. I cried and told him to be strong—that I would see him later. He was uncomfortable and kept moaning in his sleep. I could not believe he just had surgery on his little ears. Finally, he came to, and I held him and told him all was OK. He would, we hoped, not have all those awful ear infections again.

Life moved quickly those next few years. We drove to Vegas a lot. My uncle from Australia, Brian (I loved the name and asked my mom if she was okay with our naming our son, Brian; she gave us her blessing), was coming in to spend time with his sisters, my mom, and his younger sister who lived just two doors from my parents. It was fun listening to his accent. Even though he was from England like my mother, he emigrated to Australia in the 1950s.

One day I noticed all my wooden spoons were missing from the kitchen drawer. We had bought Brian a backpack, as he had seen other children with them. I started to notice how heavy it was, and one night after he and Michael were asleep, I looked through it. There, inside, were all my wooden spoons, his favorite toys, and stuffed animals. Jim and I laughed so hard, we both almost busted a lung. We used a wooden spoon to slap his back leg when he was pounding on the window or doing something we considered dangerous.

On the weekends, we would take the boys to the park or beach. We loved taking them to the zoo as well as Griffith Park in their strollers. Brian refused and loved walking and running around. We took them to Train Town, and they loved the trains. It was so much fun exploring our city and all the wonderful places to visit with young children.

One weekend on a Sunday, my day to sleep in, Brian and Michael came into our room, bounced on the bed, and wanted to go play outside. It was only 7:00 a.m. and way too early. Jim got out of bed to get his robe and was having an argument with Brian about why it was too early to play outside. Brian was exasperated and kept saying it was not, and he and his brother wanted to go outside. Jim finally said for the tenth time "NO." Brian looked up at his dad, who was standing naked, and said to him, "I am going to rip off your meatball and flush it down the toilet!" Wow! Jim and I tried so hard not to laugh, but it was so funny seeing this little guy telling his father what he was going to do.

Brian had a way about him that was just so darn cute.

He never did rip off his dad's private parts and did not go out to play that early. Jim made them breakfast, and they went outside at a decent time, around 9:00 a.m. That memory is forever embedded in our minds. Jim and I both loved being parents to these little creatures and were always in awe of what they would say next. We both understood why couples have more than three or four children. When children are growing and learning their world and exploring, it is just so precious.

There were weekends we just stayed home and let the boys run around naked in the backyard. They both loved having no clothes on. What kids don't? Jim was so good with them while I made breakfast, lunch, and dinner. It really was a time in my life that I wish did not go so fast. Seeing my little men grow up was heartwarming and joyful. Jim and I are avid readers, so we wanted to instill that in our boys. We read to them every night, and each boy would bring one or two books before bed. Brian loved Dr. Seuss, and Michael loved Berenstain Bears.

When Brian was almost three and potty trained, we enrolled him in Pinecrest preschool. It was time for him to be around children his own age and time for just Michael and me for a few hours. Brian loved getting dressed by himself. Of course, the first time I left him, he did not like that at all. By the end of the week, he really liked it and would kiss me bye-bye and go with the teacher. I could not believe how grown up he was—talking in full sentences and being very observant of his surroundings. Brian just seemed to know things without having Jim or me explain. Perhaps reading to him every night paid off, one can only hope!

I had time with Michael, and we ran errands together and played. It was mommy-and-me time for Michael now. If I had errands to run and needed to go without Michael, Mary and Jack would take him for a few hours.

Brian turned three while being at school, so I took a clown cake for all the class. It was so much fun, and all the children loved the cake. That night, we took both boys to Chuck E. Cheese. Transformer toys were big, and Brian could transform those suckers so fast it made my head spin. He had such good hand-eye control. He would help Michael with them and was actually speaking for his brother. We had to ask him to let Michael talk, but sometimes we could not understand Michael. He seemed to speak a different language that only Brian knew.

In January 1987, we attempted to take our boys to Disneyland but it started to rain, so we stopped in downtown Los Angeles at the children's museum instead. We got lunch and walked around the museum with both boys. We were getting tired and could see they were as well. We stopped to get souvenirs. I was holding onto Brian and Jim onto Michael. He reached in his pocket for his wallet, and Michael was gone. My heart fell to my stomach. Oh my God, where could he be? We both thought, "Oh no, he went into the elevator." All of a sudden we heard his laughter and spotted him. Jim and I were so relieved. It was one of the scariest moments of our lives. Thank God he was not in the elevator.

We finally made Disneyland the following weekend and had a blast. We went on all the rides the kids wanted to go on, had lunch and dinner, and got home very late with two tired sons.

The next few years flew by, and in 1989 Brian was in kindergarten. Jim and I agreed that for grade school the boys would go to Catholic school. Brian had tons of friends, as did Michael since he was now at Pinecrest as well. Brian met a wonderful boy, Joey on the first day. Joey was Korean, and they became buddies. Brian told us his teacher asked the class who would like to be friends with Joey, and Brian raised his hand. Children are so special, as they don't see color or race like adults.

Pinecrest had several lovely field trips for the children that year, and being a stay-at-home mom, I had the opportunity to be included to help the teacher. I loved being there for Brian, and he was proud that his mom could help and supervise. I vividly remember the pumpkin patch and the Tree People. I was honored that the teacher liked me and always asked if I could come help—great memories.

That year we got to know Joey and his family. We used to have Joey over for sleepovers, and Brian would go over to his house. Michael had lots of friends as well; both of my boys were very social and thus began life with getting to know other parents and lots of sleepovers. In addition to sleepovers, there were always birthday parties to attend. Both of our sons were well-liked by their peers.

The summer of 1989, we were invited to attend a barbecue at my friend Sandie's house in the Hollywood Hills. She had a lovely pool and Jacuzzi. The boys were splashing in the water, and I saw them go to the Jacuzzi. There were several people in the hot tub. After a few seconds, I did not see my Michael, and there he was in the middle of the Jacuzzi. I pulled my baby out, and he coughed and spurted. I did not make a big deal of it, but I had nightmares for months about my Michael drowning. Shortly after that, I enrolled them in swimming lessons at the YMCA in North Hollywood. Naturally, Michael was afraid at first of the water, but the teacher was very comforting, and he eventually learned how to swim. By the end of the first lesson, Brian was swimming to the other side. It took Michael longer, but he did well. It was the best money we spent.

We put the boys in soccer, and Jim was an assistant coach for Brian. It was so much fun seeing the boys on the field not knowing what the heck to do. They quickly learned teamwork and how the game worked.

Jim was interested in getting the boys in Cub Scouts as well. That was fun for Jim, doing all the crafts and pinewood derbies. We always had a lot of fun with the boys and other families. Jim took them camping and to the beach for several outings.

In the fall of 1989 there were ads on TV for Santa's Village in San Bernardino. Brian asked us to take them one weekend, as he and Michael wanted to go. The ads were adorable. Brian loved to repeat the ad: "Children, have your parents take you to Santa's Village in the crisp cool mountains of San Bernardino." It was a lot of fun, and we took lots of pictures of the boys enjoying the rides, eating caramel apples, and running around. We wore them out, and they both slept all the way home.

At Christmas, we got the boys a Nintendo, and Brian had fantastic hand-eye control. Michael was afraid and just watched Brian trying to figure it all out. I tried some of the games when the boys went to bed and did not have good hand-eye control at all! After that, Joey would come over, and he and Brian competed, and again Michael just watched. Before the end of the year, Michael was a pro at the games, and then he and Brian would play.

Brian started first grade in 1990 at St. John Baptist De La Salle School in Granada Hills. He was a model student. He loved learning and would come home and tell me all he learned that day. Michael was in kindergarten at Pinecrest. There were lots of half days at school for Brian, so he and I would go to the movies or lunch. I remember taking Brian to see *Home Alone* and how he laughed during the scene of the ice on the steps and the hot iron. We promised to take Dad and Michael on the weekend. Brian laughed himself silly seeing it again!

One day, after I picked Brian up on one of his half days, he was upset because I would not buy him a toy. If you saw the boys' room, you would think it was a toy store. He was so angry with me that he threatened to run away from home. I was quite taken aback at his anger, and then he said "I hate you." That hurt me, so I said, "If you want to run away, then you have to take off all your clothes. You came into this world naked, and you will have to go naked." He looked at me and ran into his room, took off all his clothes, opened the front door, and looked out. I said, "Go on. You don't love me anymore. See if you can find a new mommy that is better than me." He looked at me, closed the door, and ran into his room.

    I gave him a few minutes and then went in to see what he was doing. He was lying in bed with the covers over his head. I sat down and said, "Are you and I OK now?" He held out his arms to me and said, "I am sorry, Mommy." He was such a sweet soul and so loving. How could I possibly stay mad at him? Brian was so special and so kind to his friends and to his brother. He had something that I just adored—a kindness and gentleness about him. He deeply cared for those less fortunate, even at age six. He loved school and just loved learning new and different things. I remember making the boys' lunches for school. I would write little notes telling them how much mommy loved them and to have fun and enjoy school. I never asked the boys about those little notes, nor did they ever say anything to me about them. I knew they knew how special they were and how much they were loved.

Chapter Three
1991–1995

Most of our summers were spent going to see my parents in Vegas. The boys loved their cousin, Jesse, who lived with my parents. Sometimes we would go to San Diego for a weekend or Santa Barbara. The boys loved the beach, and their favorite was Leo Carrillo in Malibu. The tide pools were their absolute favorite to explore. We loved walking with the boys up and down the beach to watch the boats or surfers on the water. I would make tuna fish sandwiches, and we would eat after the boys were tired of the water for a few minutes. Those days were so beautiful and fun. We would sing in the car on the way or play games.

I had discovered San Luis Obispo before I met Jim and wanted to go back to my favorite place, the Apple Farm Inn. We took the boys one weekend and ate there and bought toys at the gift shop for them. We would walk the sand dunes in Pismo afterward. If we did not want to go that far, we would just head to Santa Barbara, find a hotel, and walk along the pier and watch the crowds. The boys loved to play in the water and body surf. Those family outings are forever embedded in my mind. It went too fast.

I think because Brian was the oldest, and only thirteen months older, Michael followed his big brother. They became such good friends and played together, even when one would have a friend sleep over. Conversely, if Michael did not have a sleepover to attend, Brian always asked if his brother could come. It was just so sweet how much they loved each other and how well they played together. I never heard them yell or scream at each other or have fistfights.

When we did have sleepovers, both boys understood that their friends had to mind me or they would not be invited back. One friend of Michael's was definitely not invited back. He kept asking Michael why, and Michael told me he told him, "You did not mind my mother." That was the end of that. I explained to the boys that when they spent the night at someone's house, I hoped they were polite and minded the mom and dad. I never once had complaints about them. Jim and I were always complimented about how polite and kind they were. Can we take credit?

The summer before Michael was to start first grade and Brian was entering second grade, the boys expressed an interest in acting. We enrolled them in an acting school in Burbank for six weeks that was on Saturdays. Perfect, it gave Jim and I time alone for lunch and to catch up on being a couple. The boys both enjoyed the acting school immensely. We got headshots of both of them and got an agent. Brian did get a small part in a B movie, and Michael got some music videos and a Nintendo commercial.

After a while, they decided the auditions were too much and both quit. At least they had the experience, which I am most grateful for.

Michael started first grade, and Brian went into second. Later in the school year, it was time for Brian to make his first Holy Communion. It was so fun hearing Brian come home and tell us about what he was learning in religion class and how excited he was. We had lost touch with his godparents, and he was interested in talking to them. I called Judy; she and Brian spoke for several minutes. He just wanted to speak to his godmother. Bless his heart!

That Christmas, we got the boys bikes and started to teach them to ride them. Brian was adamant that he did not want training wheels. So Jim took the training wheels off. Though Brian kept falling, he never once cried. He was determined to ride that bike no matter what. At the end of the day, he was riding like a champ. Michael, being more cautious, stayed with the training wheels for quite some time.

Brian made his Communion on Saturday, May 9, 1992. My mom and Jesse came for the ceremony, and we all went out to lunch afterward. I can still see him in his white shirt, black tie, and black pants. He was so adorable with his hands together in prayer. I was so grateful that it was a beautiful day.

The rest of 1992 was a bit of a blur. In 1993, Michael made his First Communion in May, and again the Lord blessed us with a beautiful day. Jesse would spend some of his summers with us those years. The boys loved him like an older brother, and they all got along. Jesse truly was like a son to Jim and me. We loved him, and he knew his Aunt Janet and Uncle Jim were always there for him.

Brian was forever negotiating with us when we both said "no" to something he wanted. He was good, and both of us agreed that Brian could think quickly on his feet. We used to say to him, "Oh, God—just what the world needs, another lawyer."

We took them to San Diego and the zoo one weekend, and Brian told us how much he liked San Diego. The Pacific

Coast Highway is a beautiful drive. We found a fabulous restaurant in San Clemente called El Adobe and would stop there to eat on the way. The boys loved the zoo and all the animals, especially the baboons. One night when we stayed in San Diego, we went to Red Lobster. Brian looked at the menu, as did Michael. Brian told us he wanted lobster. I looked at him and said, "I am not having lobster, nor are you." He demanded lobster, but Jim said to him to order something else: lobster is out of the price range. Brian thought ordering off the children's menu was beneath him. He had expensive taste even then.

Early on the morning of January 17, 1994, it felt like our world was ending. The noise was so loud, and the shaking was like a 747 landing in our house. It literally knocked Jim out of bed. He was trying to stand when the shaking stopped. We both got up and ran to the kids' rooms. Both were sound asleep in their bottom bunk. Neither of us could believe it. The TV was knocked on the floor, broken into a million pieces. The strange thing was, the boys were both spending the night out with one of Michael's friends when Michael called for us to come get him at 10:00 p.m. He wanted to come home, and so did Brian. Since there wasn't any school the next day, we agreed. Did our Michael have a premonition? I wonder sometimes. At the time, both boys were enjoying sleeping on the floor, like camping out. That night, when Jim came back with them, he said, "No. Sleep in your beds." Of course, they both slept on the bottom bunk, and neither woke up for the earthquake.

The boys sure felt the aftershocks, but neither was scared because we remained calm. Our neighbors and us all came together to assist each other and make sure we were alive and well. That morning at 4:30 a.m. is when it struck, and it seemed like it took forever for the sun to rise that morning to assess the damage. At that point, we did not care as long as our family was safe.

It took a few days for my sister, Diane, in Riverside to reach us. She asked how we were and if I could call Mom. She was worried.

I did get in touch with my mother later the second day; she was on pins and needles, worried about us. I told her what had happened with the sleepover and the sleeping on the floor. She thanked God for our Michael calling to come home with Brian. It was so hot outside after the quake, a rarity in January. I asked Mom if she would not mind having us for a visit since the boys were out of school that week for damage to the school and church.

Driving to Vegas with only me, Brian, and Michael in the car was nice. Just the three of us—singing and playing games along the way. They were excited about being off of school and seeing their cousin, Jesse. I told them that Jesse would be in school, so they would have to wait for him to come home to play. They were patient, and my mom and I kept them occupied. It was a very pleasant visit; we were just sorry that Jim had to work and help his parents.

Joey and his family moved to Orange County not long after the earthquake. We were all sad because Joey was like a third son. Brian and he promised to stay in touch.

Jim had vacation in March 1994, and we were invited to Denver to visit my best friend, Cindi, and her husband, Bill. Cindi and I met in Vegas prior to my moving to California; we worked together and had remained best friends ever since. She and Bill lived on the edge of Denver in Lakewood. I had always wanted to drive and see Utah and Colorado. We packed up our minivan and drove first to Vegas and spent the night with my parents. The next day, we started early and got to see the "purple mountain majesties" in Utah. It was just beautiful. The boys read and slept while Jim and I talked about how fabulous it was to see the beauty all around us. It had rained and was just magnificent. We stopped in Grand Junction that night. Trying to find food was quite difficult; remember we had no GPS at that time and had to drive around. That morning, we got breakfast and left for Denver.

We stopped halfway from Grand Junction to Denver for a break and a little picnic. The air was crisp and so fresh in the Rockies. We got to Cindi's late that afternoon and could not find one of Michael's shoes that we had just bought for the trip. We looked everywhere and finally figured it fell out of the van at the picnic area. Off to the shoe store we went to buy more shoes.

Cindi and Bill were perfect hosts. They had three bedrooms upstairs and a huge den downstairs. It was a lovely home: brand new and nicely decorated. The kids had the whole downstairs and a huge sofa to sleep on. We took the boys to Cheyenne one day to show them where I had gone to school and lived as a child. We bought some souvenirs and had a blast that day. The next day it snowed, so the boys played in the snow and had a fabulous time making a snowman with Bill and Jim. Cindi and I got to visit and go out a few times by ourselves while the boys played games. Cindi and Bill took us to a Rookies game, and we ate hot dogs and enjoyed the game immensely. Bill, being a schoolteacher in Alaska, was so great with the boys. He enjoyed teaching them new games and playing with them.

I promised Jim a visit to the largest bookstore in Denver. If my memory serves me, it was the Tattered

Cover Book Store. Jim and I took turns with Brian and Michael while they looked at books and toys. What a truly magnificent bookstore. We must have stayed there for several hours.

Unfortunately, the week went by fast, and it was time to start the drive home. We left very early and decided to drive straight to Vegas and stay the night with my parents. It would be twelve or thirteen hours with a few stops for gas and toilet breaks. We did it and managed to stay a few days with Mom and Dad. All in all, it was a fantastic trip with lots of memories.

In 1995, Jim's mom suffered a stroke and was hospitalized for a week. Jim's brother, Andy, came in from Utah, and they both helped their dad and mom. I knew Jim would have to spend more time with his mom and dad, so I understood.

That same year my mom was diagnosed with a tumor on her right lung. Oh boy, what a year 1995 was turning out to be for Jim and me. I flew back as often as I could, and my dad kept me informed. Surgery was scheduled to remove the tumor. We all waited—my dad, Gail, and me—for the doctor to give us the news. We were all so grateful when the doctor came out to tell us all was well, and my mom should make a full recovery.

Mid-1995 we moved to the Santa Clarita Valley and took the boys out of Catholic school and put them in public school. We had heard the schools were good, and both boys wanted to go. We enrolled them in Stevenson Ranch Elementary, and they both agreed it was nice not wearing uniforms. Brian was in sixth grade and Michael in fifth.

Chapter Four

1996–1999

B rian asked us one weekend if he could go visit Joey, and we made arrangements with Joey's mom. It was quite a drive for all of us, but we arranged to meet halfway. Brian stayed the weekend with Joey, and we met again halfway. Brian loved Korean food, and we know how much Joey loved "American food." Jim and I were so happy they kept in touch; what a wonderful friendship.

I remember parent-teacher conferences and was never more proud of Brian. His teacher told Jim and me that he was very well-liked by all the students in class. She then said, "Brian knows exactly where he fits in the universe. He is helpful in class and does his work. You are both doing an amazing job with your son." I was beaming with pride and was happy to hear such a good report. It was so true what my mother said when she first met Brian, that he'd been here before. He was definitely an old soul and just seemed to be more aware than the rest of us.

Our Michael on the other hand was having behavioral issues. He could not sit still and was being disruptive in class. He was the class clown and liked attention. We had to have numerous talks with him about being respectful in class to the teacher and other students.

Both boys had a plethora of friends. Jim and I liked having their friends over to our house for pizza or to just hang out. I made sure we had all the parents' phone numbers and they had ours. I made a list of them to put on the refrigerator.

Brian went to La Mesa Junior High in seventh grade and was very studious. I loved the fact that he always did his homework first before going outside and playing. Brian liked to pace like his father; I started to see where the carpet was getting worn. He was very good about letting me know where he was going in the neighborhood and who he was with. We had our disagreements, although for the most part Brian was respectful. He did like to try and negotiate as he did as a child.

The Christmas of 1997, Brian wanted a skateboard, so of course we got him one. He was good at it, and all his friends had them. He liked doing turns and loops—whatever they are called. It scared me, but as Jim said, "Boys will be boys," scrapes and all.

Brian made a lot of friends at school, and there were quite a few socials. I found that Brian loved to dance and go to parties at several of his friends' houses. He and Ashley became friends and were sort of going out, although seventh grade is too young to date. They were always chaperoned.

Eighth grade rolled around, and Brian continued to excel in school; his grades were all straight As. He took Spanish in school and learned the language very quickly. He had a knack for language and the arts. His drawings were amazing. He could draw anything. Neither Jim nor I are artistic and wondered where it came from. We finally discovered it was from Jim's brother, Andy.

At eighth grade graduation, Brian won the presidential award signed by President Clinton. We were so surprised and proud of our son. We are happy that Jim's mom was able to be present for that award, although in a wheelchair. Brian was just a joy to be with, and we could see how his classmates adored him. We all went out after that to celebrate. Mimi loved going out, and her favorite restaurant was Red Lobster. The boys loved it as well. Brian developed a taste for lobster and crabs. Unfortunately, my parents could not make it but were there in spirit.

At this time, Michael was much taller and bigger than Brian. Brian seemed OK with his younger brother being taller; he had the self-esteem and confidence that even though his younger brother was taller, he was still older.

That summer of 1998, we went to Redding to visit Jim's best friend and his best man at our wedding in 1983. We had a week off, and it was a very hot July in Redding that summer. Stan had a pool, and his wife, Amelia, was pregnant with their first child. Stan had a huge piece of property and took the boys out on his quads all over the property. The boys had such fun with Jim and Stan. They also had two dogs that were adorable and loved swimming in the pool.

After a few days there and the heat, we drove down to Monterey and got an ocean-view room to cool off. We took the kids to the aquarium, but they seemed to not care much for that, as there was an arcade across the street. They preferred playing games, so we let them do that after they had seen enough of the aquarium. We had a nice reprieve in Monterey and then headed home.

Brian was starting high school and would be attending Valencia High School that year. I believe he was excited and met more boys his age in the neighborhood. He had a nice group of friends that came over who were very respectful. I remember Ryan, Brandon, and Tommy—all brothers, with Tommy being the oldest. They were the nicest boys, and I was grateful that Brian met them, along with Danny, Matt, and another Ryan. There were so many I could not keep track of. I did manage to get all their parents' phone numbers so I could find Brian when needed.

At this time, Michael was really acting up. Jim and I had to pick him up at school a lot because of his behavior. My poor baby was just not himself and seemed to be having some mental issues. One day after school, he took a knife to me and threatened to cut me into little pieces. I calmly stood there (even though he was much taller than me) and stared him down. He finally put the knife down and went outside to play. I was shaking like a leaf; I called Jim and asked him to please come home. Before he left work, he spoke to his HR about what we should do.

We had to hospitalize him, and UCLA was on the list for our insurance. He stayed there for almost a week while we drove back and forth to see the doctors and figure out what was happening to our baby. It broke my heart to see him there, and all they were trying to do to help him. He looked like he was losing his mind and was saying weird stuff to the doctors. We were questioned about my pregnancy, drug use, etc. It was so upsetting for both Jim and me. Jim remembered how I grieved for my brother during Michael's pregnancy, but neither of us used drugs.

It was finally mentioned that—with the severity of Michael's condition and all the medications they tried on him— maybe residential placement was for the best. He needed constant supervision and lots of therapy to help him. We as a family needed to attend those sessions as well to help Michael become well. Thank goodness we moved to the Santa Clarita Valley, as the district was excellent in helping us get our baby the help he needed.

Jim and I are forever grateful for Hathaway Children and Family Services in Tujunga. Michael was placed there and lived there while Jim, Brian, and I went every week for therapy. It was eye-opening for all of us. We found out a lot of things about ourselves and what we could do to help our son.

About this time, Brian said he wished for an older brother. I told him that he had his cousin, Jesse, and to be grateful for that. He said it was not the same. I remember saying, "Sweetheart, why don't you be the older brother to Michael that you wished you had?" It just came out of my mouth, and Brian looked at me with those gorgeous chocolate-brown eyes and said, "Right!" I knew he understood what I meant. He was an old man at times and like my mom said "an old soul."

Brian started high school, and we got into a routine. Tuesdays we had to drive to Tujunga for therapy and to see our Michael. On Saturdays, we could take him out for lunch for an hour or so. Our life was certainly interesting, learning new ways to cope with Michael not living with us.

Brian thrived at high school. He had so many friends, it was hard to keep track. I was just happy he was doing OK, even with his brother not living with us. He never complained about going to therapy with us, nor did he blame Michael. He just went with the flow. I would talk to him about how it was affecting him, and he was sad for his brother but understood he needed help. As always, his homework came first before going out to visit friends. On Saturdays, if Brian was busy with friends, we would go by ourselves to take Michael out to lunch. Michael always asked where Brian was, and we always told him the truth: he was out with friends. We always told him that Brian loved him and would see him on Tuesday. Michael had gained a lot of weight with the medication they had him on, although he did seem calmer and more in control of his behavior. We really liked all the teachers and counselors and felt it was a safe environment for our son.

Early in 1999, Brian asked if I would take him and a friend, Ryan, to Wrightwood to go snowboarding. I remember it was a long weekend with Martin Luther King Jr. Day. We also had Michael for the long weekend, which was perfect. I agreed, and even though it was raining, the boys still wanted to go. Brian was a good snowboarder, and so was Ryan. Michael and I dropped them off and went exploring the town and ate at a café. I had a cell phone and had gotten Brian one to keep in touch. It was freezing outside, and I know the skiing could not have been good. But Brian and Ryan wanted to stay. It was a long day when we finally left with all three boys asleep in the car.

Our friends Cindi and Bill had moved back to Alaska and invited us to visit during the summer. We were delighted with the invitation and planned to visit in June of 1999. We had to see if we could sign Michael out for a week or so and if Jim could take the time off. Of course, Michael could come home for Christmas for a week or so, which was great. We all went to visit my family in Vegas and had a fabulous time as always. My mother and I had always had a special bond; Brian and Michael loved being there and absolutely loved their nana and pop-pop and, of course, Jesse. Jim and my father always talked about books, and we all had an enjoyable time.

Soon, it was time to leave for our trip to Alaska. Flights were booked, and we had a car service pick us up. I know our sons were very excited because both had read about the wilderness and what to expect. Cindi promised to take us to see glaciers and some of the small towns, as she was taking the week off work. She and Bill lived in Anchorage. Bill had lived through the Alaskan earthquake in 1964.

We arrived at 11:50 p.m. from LAX to Anchorage. How do you explain that the sun was still up and shining this late at night? It was just beautiful seeing the huge horizon and breathing in the crisp air. I knew before our vacation began that this was going to be a truly remarkable experience for all of us.

Cindi picked us up and took us to her home with Bill. It was so nice to be there. The boys adored Bill and Cindi. We all sat outside until 2:00 a.m. and still could not believe the sun was up, like it was going down but would come right back up. We all finally went to bed and slept in late.

Bill promised the boys he would take them fishing one day, and Cindi promised to take us all around the city and to Earthquake Park. One or two days were for Cindi and me to get out and leave the boys and men to their own devices.

One beautiful morning, Cindi drove us to a park with gold panning. The boys really got into that and had fun. We saw goats on the side of a hill and then went to a river with a glacier. We stopped and took some great pictures, and that's when I saw a baby cub. I so wanted to pet it, but Jim pulled my jacket and told me mama bear is not far. We all hiked back another way, not before I got a picture though. When we arrived back to Cindi's, we had to stop for a moose crossing the street. Now, that is something you don't see every day! We all had to take a picture as the moose was very slow indeed.

Cindi and I took the train one day to Whittier and a cruise around a glacier. It was amazing how you could hear the crackling of the glacier when the boat stopped. We could see bears and eagles way off. It was absolutely so beautiful and untouched. I felt such a sense of spirituality being there. I was a bit sad that the boys and Jim had not come, but I knew they were having fun with Bill fishing.

We were so busy that week, and it flew by. Our last night before heading back home, Cindi made a fantastic seafood dinner. I mean really! She had lobster, crab, halibut, cod, and swordfish. Brian deemed it the best meal he ever had! After being gone a week, it felt like we were gone months.

There was much to do to get Michael ready to head back to Hathaway. Brian would be starting tenth grade and wanted a job so he could have his own money. He was doing his own washing and helping around the house, but still, a young man wants his own money.

One day, he headed out to Granary Square and asked every store owner if he could work for them. He found out he had to be sixteen, and he would not be until March 2000. He did try, and I will always be so proud of that. We upped his allowance and told him before he knew it he would be sixteen.

At the end of 1999, I mentioned to Jim that we were outgrowing the house we had; it was too small for us with two big, growing boys. When they walked down the hall, one had to step aside for the other. We started looking and found a two-story house with four bedrooms, three bathrooms, and a pool. Brian chose the bedroom downstairs and Michael the bedroom upstairs. That left a room for Jim and me to finally have an office at home.

One day Brian had gone for a run around the neighborhood. Always health conscious, he was into taking care of his body. He and Jim would get into it about Jim's belly. I remember Jim saying to Brian, "Just you wait. When you are my age, it will happen to you too, and I pray I live long enough to see it." Brian retorted, "That will never happen to me, old man." Jim and I laughed at each other.

Anyway, I digress. Brian went for a run, and it seemed an hour later, he walked in with a huge goose egg on his forehead and a swollen eye. I immediately got an ice pack while he told me some guy had started punching him. I called the police, and an officer seemed to be at the door in no time. Brian reported what happened. After that, Jim took Brian for boxing lessons, and he was recruited for Golden Gloves. It seemed everything Brian did, he gave it his all. He excelled in whatever he put his mind to. His drawings were amazing, and he was speaking Spanish like it was his first language.

Chapter Five

2000–2005

As 1999 moved toward 2000, there were so many fearful people of Y2K, the concern that a computer coding issue would cause widespread, serious problems. Jim and I did not believe anything would happen, but so many were fearful—it was all over the news. I really was not scared and felt all would be well. All was okay, as we are all still here!

We were scheduled to close escrow in March 2000 for our new home. Brian would finish tenth grade at Valencia High School and then transfer to Hart High School. He had a friend drive him to school, and sometimes I would take him. At this time, he started wanting to learn to drive. He asked me to show him, and on the weekends we would go up to the high school and drive around in the parking lot. He was anxious to get a car and a job, being so independent and all.

Michael was continuing on at Hathaway School since we all agreed that he was excelling there. The smaller classrooms were a bonus for him, and he felt comfortable there. He took a bus to school and got home around 4:00 p.m. every day.

On Brian's sixteenth birthday, we were packing but still

took him out to dinner and promised once we were settled in the new house, he could have a pool party. He really did not care about that; he was so good at helping us pack up, and it seemed he was excited about the move.

We moved into our new home on Jim's birthday, March 19, 2000, and we had movers do all the heavy work for us. By the time the kids came home from school, most of the furniture was in place, and they got to fix up their rooms. It was fun having a larger house—more privacy for all of us.

One day Brian came in the door and said, "Guess what?" I was curious and of course said, "What?" Brian said, "Our next door neighbor is my junior high school principal." I remembered Rochelle and how eloquently she spoke at the graduation when Brian had won the presidential award. Small world, eh?

We promised Brian a car, and since he got his license, we started looking for cars for him. He was continuing to look for a part-time job. He found one as a bag boy at Ralphs in Stevenson Ranch, so he did need a car to get back and forth from school and work. We found an ad in the Pennysaver for an Oldsmobile Cutlass, but it was all the way in Lake Elizabeth. It was in our price range. We had Brian tell us what he wanted, and of course he wanted a sports car! But he was reasonable about a car and decided he wanted to see it. We called and made an appointment. I made sure we had cash in case he wanted it; he and Jim could drive it home. Michael came with us, and that's when he told me he was not interested in driving until he was eighteen. He did ask me to teach him when he was sixteen though.

Brian liked the car, and he and the owner checked under the hood, as Brian was in auto shop class at school. He was excited. We paid the guy, got the title, and waved goodbye. Jim drove with Brian; I drove with Michael. When we got home, we expressed to Brian that California law was that he could not have anyone under twenty-one in his car for the next six months. He promised to abide by the law. We trusted him, as he never gave us any reason not to. He always seemed to have his act together, and his grades were excellent. I can candidly say I never worried about Brian; he knew right from wrong. I was always proud of his report cards and his academic achievements in school. His art and writing were so profound for such a young man. Sometimes, he acted like he was so much older than he was. An old soul, just like my mom said.

Brian came up to me one day after we got the car for him and hugged me, thanking me for all we had done for him. I was touched and told him how much I loved him and that there wasn't anything his dad and I would not do for him. All he had to do was ask.

Now that he had his car, he could go see Joey in Orange County. He did and was always back when he said he would be. It was so nice to see this friendship that had lasted since kindergarten continue.

Drinking was a concern for all parents. Jim and I did not intend to be the "cool" parents, but we did tell our boys that if they were to drink, to do it at home. We allowed them a small glass of beer from time to time and encouraged them to call us and not drive home if they drank at a friend's house. Brian had heard of classmates drinking and driving and getting killed while driving in canyons. He assured us he had a good head on his shoulders.

I remember those days back in the 1970s when Mothers Against Drunk Driving (MADD) was formed. So many lives were lost due to drinking and driving. It was refreshing when coffee bars like Starbucks started up. Instead of drinking alcohol, we all were into caffeine.

After our move, life seemed busy fixing up the house and going back and forth to see my parents. It was an interesting time of being in a new century (although technically it wasn't until January 1, 2001 according to *Jeopardy*).

September in 2000, Jim and I had a wedding to attend in Malibu, and since Michael was home full time now, we asked Jim's mom and dad if he could spend the night with them. Brian, being sixteen, we trusted to stay home. He asked if he could have a few friends over, and Jim and I agreed, but only a few.

Well, when we got home that night, we thought we were in the twilight zone. Our garage was full of cars, and there were no parking spaces anywhere close to our house. I truly thought we were on the wrong street. No, this was our house, kids coming in and out. Jim dropped me off, and I went into the house completely dumbfounded. I cannot even say how many kids were in our house. I walked around, and that's when Jim came in and shouted, "PARTY IS OVER." We found Brian, and he could hardly stand still; he was plastered.

The kids scrambled out like cockroaches—so fast you blinked and they were gone. There were beer cans everywhere, including the pool. The barbecue was on, and cigarette butts were everywhere. I was in a state of shock and was so angry at Brian. I yelled at him and told him to clean it up and that he was not going to bed until my house was as I left it.

Looking back, it was funny but not at the time. He told a few friends and, of course, it went around the whole school. Whenever we spoke about it, we all laughed. Kids!

That December, we all decided to go to Big Bear as Brian wanted to snowboard, and I found a nice three-bedroom, two-bath home to rent for four days. Our nephew, Jesse, was in Riverside at the time, so we picked him up on the way to Big Bear. Poor Michael, his feet were too big for snowshoes. He did not get to go with Brian and Jesse, but we managed to find things for him to do. The house came equipped with a lot of games to play, and we had a fabulous time. I have great memories of Jesse and Brian coming down the slopes.

The year 2001 was technically the start of the new millennium. That April, my sister Cathy passed away suddenly at age forty. I went to support my mom and dad and was so upset that now they had lost two children out of six. It was so very heartbreaking to see my parents lose yet another child.

What a year it was, especially on September 11, 2001. I truly don't think anybody will forget where they were that day when they heard. It was just shocking! Life as we knew it had come to an end that day. Watching the news and the planes hitting the towers was unspeakable, knowing there were innocent people on the planes and in those buildings. There just aren't any words.

That fall, Brian came home one night and expressed a desire to join the Marines and asked if we would sign for him to join now. Both Jim and I agreed he might change his mind before he turned eighteen. Jim expressed his desire that Brian go in the service as an officer and not an enlisted man. Brian, as always, was adamant and negotiated with us. I finally said, "No, I will not sign for you. If you still want to join after you graduate that is your decision. I will not sign for you while you are seventeen because you may change your mind, and if I sign, you would be committed to join." A few weeks later, I received a call from a Marine recruiter asking me to sign for Brian. I told the recruiter the same thing I told Brian. The recruiter then said that after four years, Brian's college would be paid for. I said, "We can afford college for our son." The recruiter did say how lucky we were to be able to afford college for Brian. That was the end of that.

In December of that year, Jim's father passed away in his sleep. It's always a blessing to hear of a passing in their sleep. No suffering—you just leave this plane for another. We were sad for Jim's mom, as they had been together for over sixty years.

I had decided to donate a kidney to a lady I had met in 1998. I had always felt it was something I had to do. We were getting close to all the tests being done at UCLA, and surgery was set for January 2002. Jim was okay with it, and I told the boys. Nobody objected, except my mother. After the surgery, my mom sent me yellow roses and just wanted to make sure I was doing fine.

Brian, Jim, and Michael came to visit me in the hospital, and Brian told me he had been hired at a restaurant at the mall, Sisley. He was really excited about being hired. I was very proud of him, as long as it did not interfere with his school. He had quit the job at Ralphs when he was offered the job at Sisley. He liked the idea of making tips and learning more about food, especially Italian food, which was one of his favorite.

Brian graduated Hart High School that June of 2002 at the College of the Canyons stadium. It was a beautiful day, and we were so proud of our young man. Jim and I told both boys that they could take six months off after high school before furthering their education. Joining the Marines for Brian was in the past, and it was never mentioned again.

Brian started College of the Canyons that fall to get all of his prerequisites out of the way. He did mention transferring to Cal State, Northridge (CSUN) in a few years. He wanted a bachelor's degree, like his father.

That October, we took Michael out of school, and Brian got off work and school to go to Hawaii. We wanted a nice vacation together before the boys went their separate ways in life. We started in Waikiki, Oahu. The boys had a room right next to ours, and we had breakfast every day at the hotel. Both Jim and Brian were going to quit their jobs and move there, of course. I had no say in the matter. Falling in love with the Hawaiians was easy; they were so friendly and polite. We asked the boys if they wanted to do anything, and both agreed: jet skiing, parasailing, and scuba diving. We found a package for the boys and sent them off while Jim and I explored. The boys liked walking the back alleys in Waikiki and exploring noodle houses at night, rather than having dinner with us. They wanted their dad to take them shooting. Jim found a place not far from the hotel to go shooting, while I got to lie on the beach. I just loved Diamond Head and the gorgeous view from the beach. I loved the smell of the ocean and watching the surfers. The water was a brilliant blue with aquamarine hues; it was just scintillating!

After four days in Oahu, we ventured to the island of Maui. We had a lovely three-bedroom condo right on the ocean with a view of Molokai. It was just incredible. Brian and Michael wanted to explore on their own, so we rented Brian a Rent-a-Wreck car, and they did their thing. It was quite late when they got back. Being a mom, I was worried. I was glad they had a nice time. We had dinner together our last night, and the waiter took a picture of us together.

It was hard saying goodbye to such a lovely vacation and great times, but it was time for reality.

I fondly look back at that time with a smile and a heart full of love. I am grateful we had the opportunity to do that as a family and that we all got along so well. Brian was eighteen and Michael seventeen; they got along great as brothers. Jim and I often said we were so happy we had them so close in age.

On January 17, 2003, Jim's mom passed away. We were all heartbroken. Brian and Michael were very close to their grandmother. I was sad for Jim because now he was an orphan. The funeral was difficult for all of us. Brian went up to speak and lost it. I went up to get him and he just cried.

Michael graduated from Hathaway in May; we were so proud of him. He had made it through school. Hathaway had a lovely ceremony for the graduates. Our little family went to dinner afterward. As we promised, Michael could stay home and rest for six months until he decided what to do with his life. Michael got a job at Smart and Final, and we gave him a car.

In mid-January of 2004, Michael informed us he was joining the Navy. He had stopped all his medication and was becoming a young man. I was happy for him, and we all agreed it was good for him. His basic training was to be in the Chicago area. I had never been to Chicago nor had Jim. We promised Michael we would come for his graduation.

Michael went to basic training, and in April of that year, I received a call from my dad that my mom had cancer. I remember throwing the phone down; my mind could not comprehend my mother being sick. I spoke to my mom and told her I would come see her as soon as I could book a flight. She asked me not to worry and said that she loved me. I will never forget that conversation with my mom. I cried for hours that night; my eyes were so swollen I could barely see.

I told Jim and Brian about my mom, but all I could do was wait for Michael to call us. I flew to see her and was shocked at how much weight she had lost. She was not a big woman, small and petite, but her tummy was really flat, and she looked ill. I sat with her, and we talked about life and her thoughts on dying. She was given maybe six to eight months, as the cancer had spread to her brain. She knew but never said anything to anyone. I remember asking her what she felt, and she said there really wasn't any pain. I asked her if she was scared, and I can hear her words clearly, "Sweetheart, we are all afraid of the unknown."

Michael's graduation was scheduled for the end of April at Naval Station Great Lakes. Jim and I made reservations to attend and were excited to see him, although my heart was so heavy with worry about my mother. We asked Brian if he wanted to go with us but with school and work, he declined. He said Michael would understand and that he would talk to him later.

We flew into O'Hare airport and rented a car to the Drake Hotel. What a truly magnificent hotel. The room was just beautiful, with crown molding and a deep soaking tub. The next morning, we drove to Michael's graduation. Both of us were in awe that Michael stood still for so long singing the navy song. Afterward, we found out Michael had ten hours of leave. We drove back to the Drake, took him to lunch, and Jim and my baby had a cigar outside. We went to our room and called my mom. Michael got on the phone with her and then I did. I described the graduation and the hotel, and she was in good spirits.

Michael did not have to be back until 10:00 p.m. that evening. We took him to dinner at Lawry's, and he told us a funny story about his shoes. Michael is a big boy and has a size eighteen shoe. While he was attempting to get standard issue, the man helping him was astonished at the size of his feet and asked him, "What the heavens is your mom feeding you?" Michael also regaled us with stories about some of the others he had met in basic training. We were dumbfounded that so many had never been anywhere, had never seen the ocean or gone on vacations with their families. He was particularly surprised about one young man who had never even left the county he was born in. He thanked us for all the opportunities he had had with us. We had a great time at dinner, and then we drove him back to the base. He promised to come see us soon and asked us to keep him posted about his nana.

It was a lovely trip seeing Michael, and we came home and told Brian how his brother stood there for a long time without flinching. You could tell Brian was proud of his brother.

After we arrived home, it was time to go visit my mother. My sister Gail, bless her heart, was helping to take care of Mom, and I would come at the end of the week and help over the weekend so Gail could go out. Mom was very weak and was looking ashen. My dad and I suspected mom knew at the end of 2003 that she had cancer but never said anything. She never liked anybody to worry or fret about her. That's just the way she was. She was a fabulous mother, so kind and generous.

My mom's sister Maureen had flown over from England to see her. Mom's younger sister Barbara lived two doors down from them. It was nice to have all the sisters together, and we took pictures. The only ones missing were their older brother Brian and their younger half-brother Tony.

Since I had met Uncle Brian in 1986, I called and asked if he wanted to come over to see Mom, as she was very ill. Jim and I had agreed that if he could, we would pay for his trip. I know he wanted to come, but his arthritis was bad, and he said he really could not fly all that way from South Australia. He did call Mom often. Bless him.

I received a call from my mother the third week of May telling me about the wonderful surprise she had the night before. I could hear in her voice how happy she was. Her baby half-brother Tony had come to see her. Well, of course I had to meet my uncle, who was only nine years older than me. Michael got some leave, and Brian wanted to go to Vegas to see his nana as well. We all drove and were excited about meeting our relative from Manchester, England.

Mom was getting weaker, but you could tell she was happy to have all her family there. Her brother Tony was born when she was thirteen. She kept calling him her first baby. She told us stories about how he loved her and was going to marry her when he grew up. Mom and Dad asked Jim and me to take Uncle Tony out for them. We took Uncle Tony; Brian; Michael; and our friends Cindi and Bill, who were now in Las Vegas. It was a marvelous evening; though we wished Mom and Dad could have been with us.

When we got home, Tony sat with my mom, and we all took pictures. Tony could not believe the size of Michael's feet and wanted a picture to show his mates. Mom was in good spirits that night and seemed so happy to have her brother and grandsons there. Brian, Michael, and Tony got along so well, showing off their muscles and just laughing and joking as men do. My mom was also having a good time having her family around her.

Tony left at the end of May. I had the chance to tell him I would never forget what he did for my mom. He told me it's the least he could do; she was, after all, his sister.

Mom passed away on June 12th, and I was so glad I was there. I had time with her beforehand. Hospice and my sister Gail were wonderful with taking care of her. She was now at peace. Michael flew in for the celebration of life. Brian expressed how much he loved his nana and hugged me, knowing how close my mom and I were. I had lost my mom, best friend, and confident. The many gifts my mother gave and left me are all for another book to write about her amazing life in England during WWII.

In eighteen months, Jim lost both parents, and I lost my mother. It was so sad. My dad was still pretty healthy, and I wondered how long he would last. My parents had just celebrated fifty-two years of marriage.

Brian was doing well, keeping busy with work and school. He was into surfing now, and he and his friends would go to the beach. He also liked diving and found some waterfalls where he could dive. When I saw some of the videos, I was shocked. He was a real risk-taker, and I made him promise to be careful. *Not* in his vocabulary. He just loved going beyond the limit; he was intrepid! He went snowboarding in Utah with some friends, and on their last run before driving back, he hurt his shoulder and was in excruciating pain. When he got home, I put ice on it and gave him extra strength Tylenol, as I had nothing stronger. It turned out that he had a dislocated shoulder. How he managed is beyond me, but he did get better. Sometimes, I think Brian willed himself well.

It was around that time that I made a deal with him: "Brian, you are such a risk-taker and always going way beyond. I will give you $1,000 if you make it to twenty-five." Brian said, "You are on." I was really only joking, but Jim said to me, "You better pay up when he turns twenty-five."

In 2005, Brian and his friend Danny got an apartment together. Jim and I took Brian out to Anna's Linens for towels, linens, pots and pans, etc. Brian was a good cook from working at Sisley. I let him pretty much pick out what he wanted and needed.

He made me a very special dinner for my fiftieth birthday that May. It was so lovely having someone cook for me, and especially such an elegant meal—chicken penne. He even bought dessert from the restaurant. I felt like a queen. I will never forget that meal and how lovingly he prepared it for me. I was so proud of him!

Since he was working and making quite good money, Brian would buy little gifts for my birthday or Mother's Day. Since my birthday is one week after Mother's Day, it was either or but not both. That year, he made his own card for me, expressing how great a mother I am and gave me a massage gift card. I was overwhelmed by his generosity. He was so sweet and just knew what I liked.

It was just Jim and me at home now. Michael was on an aircraft carrier somewhere in the Pacific; Brian was living in an apartment with his roommate a few miles away. We had done it; we raised our boys to adulthood.

I had always wanted a baby grand piano, and when I mentioned this to Brian he said, "Yes, when can we get it?" Brian was playing guitar and being quite artistic; music was the next thing he wanted to master. So, we went out together and found one. It was just lovely, and we both agreed it would be ours; however, I had more space in my house. He agreed.

It was so lovely hearing Brian play. He sat down and just started playing once the piano arrived. I was totally amazed, as was Jim. Brian just had the tendency to do whatever he set his mind to.

Brian had transferred to CSUN and was still working at the restaurant. He still came home to raid our refrigerator whenever he could. He was so funny, always checking the pantry and refrigerator. Sometimes, he would bring his friends over to see what we had to eat. Jim and I always kept deli meats and bread in the house. I love leftovers and so does Jim, so many times, I would come home and the dinner from the night before had disappeared. Wonder where it went—Brian's stomach!

I was never angry about that but just happy he still felt comfortable coming home. If I really wanted something badly, I would mark it, "Mom's. Do not eat!" Sometimes he would be outside sunning himself or swimming in the pool. We could go on vacation and knew Brian would be there to take care of the house and finish all the food! Man, he had an appetite and could eat a full meal and still eat again an hour or so later. He worked out a lot, and his body was well defined. My friends always complimented me on how polite he was and handsome. Hearing that about your adult child is a testament to their upbringing. But in Brian's case it was his soul; he was born with a kind and loving soul.

Chapter Six

2006–2009

In 2006, Michael came home for a visit around my birthday, actually before the end of my fiftieth. I had always wanted a family photo. It was time to set it up, and we did it! We promised them a terrific lunch of their choosing; I was so proud at how they acted for the pictures. We took them to a sushi restaurant near the photo shoot location.

In November of that year, I received a call that my nephew, Jesse, had been murdered. I was devastated and immediately called Jim. I was so upset for my sister Gail. Jesse was her only child, and he was gone. Jesse was the first grandchild for my parents. I am so grateful my mother had already passed. I could visualize her being there to greet Jesse when he left this world, and that gave me comfort, but still I was so very heartbroken. Jesse was like a son to me and Jim. He was five when Brian was born. He had also spent a few summers with us when the boys were younger. They loved Jesse and were both so sad and upset when I told them that he had been murdered. We never did find out why, but the murderer was found and convicted. Gail was never the same after that.

Gail wanted a cremation for her son; Jim and I helped. We all drove to Vegas for his cremation and a small mass.

Afterward, we took our sons to dinner at the Luxor for a meal and toast to our Jesse and his life. It was bittersweet—so many losses, in such a short time, within our family.

In the early summer of 2007, Brian informed us he was giving up his apartment and was going to Europe with Tommy. He never asked if he could move back in; it just happened that way. He had saved up enough money for the trip, and they both planned three weeks away. He had already received his passport. We had a barbecue at the house for him and Tommy and all their friends before they left. I really liked Tommy's mom and stepdad. Tommy's brothers, Brandon and Ryan, came with a ton of friends. It was a wonderful send-off for the boys. Jim and I drove them to LAX airport for their big adventure!

Before Brian left, we bought him a camera and asked him to take lots of pictures. Jim had never been to Europe. I had been to England, Spain, Portugal, and Morocco when my dad was in the Air Force in the 1960s.

Brian promised and also promised to text us. Cell phones sure made life easier in some ways.

After their three weeks, Brian and Tommy came home. Tommy's family picked them up and dropped Brian off. He looked good and seemed quite happy about the trip. The first thing he said was that he was going back next year.

We could not wait to see the pictures he had taken. "Oh, yeah about the camera," he said. "I got it wet in Prague, and it did not work after that." I was so disappointed, but he did tell us about all the places they had gone. When I asked him his favorite, he said, "Innsbruck. It was just awesome standing above the city and looking at the valley below, just beautiful." Wow! I wish I had a picture of that, but I sure could visualize it in my mind.

He regaled us with stories about the trains and the people they met. He described the fresh food and how cheap some things were to eat. He described Prague and told us we had to go—it was a fabulous city with so much to do. He and Tommy were definitely going back next summer and for longer.

That Christmas, Brian requested German, Italian, Portuguese, and French for dummies. He was really into the travel bug now. We were delighted he had the means and opportunity to travel abroad. And we felt he was safe with Tommy, who was a few years older. The fact that Brian spoke fluent Spanish was also a very good thing.

That Christmas, in 2007, Michael came home. It was nice having just the four of us for dinner and gifts. I loved buying gifts for my boys. Of course, they wanted money, but I had to have something under the tree. Brian got Jim and me a beautiful painting by Thomas Kinkade, one of my favorite painters. He knew exactly the scene I wanted. I could tell how proud he was when we opened it. It was the *Garden of Prayer*. Both sons were home for Christmas, and it was a magical time for me. I loved making Christmas dinner and all the trimmings for our small family.

After dinner, both boys went out together. It was so nice seeing them getting along and still wanting to do things together. They promised that if they drank, they would call us.

The year 2008 was upon us. Brian and Tommy planned their next trip to Europe for that summer and this time were going to be gone longer. Brian was learning Portuguese and planned on getting a job at a resort in Lagos if possible so he could stay longer.

We had another little get-together before they left. Brian was short on funds and decided to sell his Tacoma truck. It was his decision, and he said when he came back he would buy something else. He never asked us for money but knew we would help if he needed it. I am glad he tried on his own.

They left that July, and I received texts here and there of where they were. Being a mother, you always worry about your children, but Jim always said to me that Brian had to have experiences of his own. They did end up in Lagos, Portugal, and Brian obtained a job as a bartender at a resort. I can only imagine the fun they were having. After a few weeks they were in Valencia, Spain for a few days, then back to Lagos. After a while, Brian texted that he bought a bike and was traveling through Germany eating off the land. Amazing! I can only imagine what my son was experiencing. I was so happy he was enjoying life and seeing different cultures and being able to speak different languages.

Brian really did learn languages easily. Spanish was so good for him to know because it helped with Italian and Portuguese. He picked up French and told me that German was really easy.

I received a text from Brian mid-August saying that he was flying home and asking if we could pick him up at LAX. He then texted the flight number and time due in. I was quite surprised that he was coming home so soon. Jim and I drove to LAX and met him at the curb. He was tired, and the first thing he did was give me a Spanish doll that I had asked him to pick up for me. Long story short, I used to collect dolls from my travels with my family, but they were all stolen. Oh well, it's only stuff. Brian told us that he would tell us what happened. Tommy was still in Europe and had met up with some other friends of theirs in Italy.

We got home, and Brian told us that he had taken a pill after working at the resort in Lagos, as he kept going back and forth to the resort from his travels. He sat on a rock looking out at the Atlantic Ocean and said if he did not keep drinking water he felt he was going to die. He had no idea what he took, but he was scared. He drank water and managed to get out of the feeling of dying and booked a flight home immediately. My heart just slammed into my stomach. We could have lost him to a drug overdose in a foreign country. I then got angry with him and asked him if he even thought about his parents and what that would do to us? All he could say was that he was sorry.

He must have slept for twelve to fourteen hours that night. We left him alone and knew when he wanted to talk, he would. Jim and I both were upset but grateful he had the sense to come home.

The next night, we took him out to sushi (his favorite) and had a great time eating and talking about his experiences in Germany. For a full day, he just ate off the land: berries, raw corn, whatever was edible. He just loved it and enjoyed the German countryside. He went to Innsbruck again to admire the beauty.

Because Brian had sold his truck for his trip, we went out looking at cars. He really did not want a car payment, or at least something not too pricey. I found something I liked and asked if he wanted my car instead, and I would get a new one. We agreed, and it all worked out well.

At the end of 2008, just before the New Year, Brian woke me up one night out of a sound sleep and asked me to stitch up his forehead. He was bleeding and definitely needed stitches. He was also very drunk and kept saying that I could stitch it up. I told him, "No way. You need to get to the emergency room right away and will most likely need a tetanus shot as well." Michael was home and still awake and offered to take hm. Before they left, I asked Brian what happened. He told me that he and one of his friends got into an argument, and the friend ran into the house and slammed the door. The door had a nail on it for a wreath, and Brian ran right into it. Of course he would need a tetanus shot and antibiotics.

That morning, I checked on Brian, and he was sound sleep with his forehead stitched up. Michael awoke first and told me that the emergency room doctor did give him a shot and several antibiotics to take.

With 2009 coming, Brian would be turning twenty-five. How often Jim and Brian reminded me of the deal I made with him about surviving to twenty-five!

On March 18th, I had cash in a birthday card for Brian. This was one day for which he could not wait. I saw him rip open the envelope. He thanked me and his dad profusely. I just hugged him and was grateful he was with us this birthday. As usual, we celebrated his and Jim's birthdays the same evening with dinner of Brian's choice. It was usually a nice restaurant that was fairly expensive and with the best food. Brian learned early on in life to eat well and play hard.

About this time, he also became interested in comedy. Brian always had a great sense of humor and made others laugh. He used to have my mother in stitches laughing so hard at his stories from the restaurant about either drunken or hungry people. There's nothing worse than a hungry person, except a drunk one. Brian would go to Hollywood to open microphone nights. Many times, I would hear him in his room rehearsing. I have to admit, he was good!

After Brian's and Jim's birthdays, my dad got sick and was not doing well. I started going back and forth to Vegas to see him. He passed away April 25, 2009 from chronic obstructive pulmonary disease (COPD). It was so hard seeing him unable to breathe. Now, I was an orphan and also the executor of his and my mom's trust. There were four of us among which to divide the household belongings. It was a very hard time for me and I know also for my sisters.

Toward the end of 2009, Brian decided to try his luck in San Francisco with comedy and a comic book he had created. He stayed with his friend Brandon for a few weeks. He bombed out and came home looking for something else. He never gave up and just found something else to move on to. I never noticed depression of any kind. He had a great attitude about life and what he wanted to experience.

Chapter Seven

2010–2015

It was hard to believe we were starting another decade of the twenty-first century. Where had the time gone?

Brian started working as a contractor with a friend of his. He did not finish his last semester at CSUN, which was disappointing for us. He was so very close—why quit now? He told us he did not feel the need for a degree. We had long talks about his career choices, and he always said the same thing, "I do not want to be tied down to a corporate career." Brian liked hiking, surfing, snowboarding, or whatever he fancied doing without punching a time clock. I had many arguments with him about his language skills and what he could do with that. Nope, he was going to do it his way. He wanted freedom, and money was not that important to him. He wanted just enough to do what he wanted to do and that was that!

I raised my boys to be independent and to try to make good choices. Once they are adults, it's their life and their choices. All a parent can do is love them and be there to support them. We were there for advice and counsel; you can only learn from your mistakes and move on.

Brian's friend Tommy would stop by a lot, and they would finish whatever leftovers we had. I really loved

Tommy and his brothers, Brandon and Ryan. They were so polite and had been coming around since Brian was in junior high.

In September of 2010, Jim and I left Brian in charge of the house while we went to Italy for two weeks. He drove us to LAX after we had a late lunch together.

Suffice to say, it was a magnificent trip but went too fast. Brian would text me often to check on us and see where we were. Italy was truly a magical place to visit and tour. The ruins were just incredible, and the history was awesome. We took a lot of pictures and agreed we would have to come back. Lake Como was an absolutely beautiful lake with a ferry to take you to the other side to visit the many small towns. Each town had its own charms; the Italians are friendly and happy people. Their country is steeped in history and a rich culture.

Venice is magical and such an awesome city to explore. Jim and I walked around in wonder at how the city was built and continued to still be here after all these centuries. Florence, a must see is Michelangelo's *David*, and later before closing is best. What a beautiful statue with mind-boggling details chiseled into the stone! How did Michelangelo do that? Truly magnificent and extraordinary.

Jim and I agreed we loved Rome. We walked around with complete wonder at the sites. One feels transported back in time by the buildings from centuries ago. The Colosseum is just stunning to see up close. You can almost hear the cheers of the people from centuries ago partaking in the sports. I wonder how many ghosts are walking around from that era. The Trevi Fountain just takes your breath away; the fountain itself is stunning to look at. We had seen pictures, but nothing compared to being there in person. Neither of us could believe that it was only one of 1,352 fountains from fourth-century Rome. One can see why this fountain stands out from the rest!

I've always been fascinated with Pompeii; never in my wildest dreams did I think I would get to actually visit this ancient city. Still being uncovered today, this city is a marvel to visit and explore.

Brian picked us up at the airport after our amazing trip! He wanted to hear all about our experiences. This time, we got to reciprocate and regale him with our stories. One thing we all agreed on, the food in Italy is so fresh, and the Italians take their time to truly enjoy their meals. I remember him saying how happy he was that we got to visit such a beautiful country.

In August of 2011, Tommy was going to Vietnam with another friend. I remember a few nights before he left he came by and told us he had just taken the bar exam. Wow! We were so proud of him. We used to think Brian would be an attorney, given the way he always negotiated with us. Tommy was several years older than Brian and a very handsome and pleasant young man. Brian was going to drive him and Tommy's friend to the airport. I wished Tommy well and said, "Don't be a stranger when you get back." He hugged me, and they left.

Three days later, I came home—I will never forget that it was a Friday—and there Brian was sitting in the den with his head down. I could tell he was really upset, and I asked him, "What's wrong, honey?" "Tommy died," he said. I said, "What? He was just here," and Brian said it was an apparent accidental overdose. I was in complete and utter shock. This can't be happening, no way. Not Tommy, such a beautiful young man—he was going to be an attorney!

Jim came home, and we told him. My heart went out to Tommy's mom, dad, brothers, sister, and grandmother. The next day, we went over with a meal to Tommy's mom's house and sat there with them and just listened. It was heartbreaking.

I had a hard time sleeping for a while after that. I kept seeing Tommy falling over and realizing he was dying and that there was nothing he could do.

Tommy had wanted to try heroin; all young men feel invincible. How awful for his whole family. He was out of the country, and his body had to be shipped back to the States. I cannot imagine all his mom, Patti, and the family were going through. I remembered Brian taking a pill in Portugal. I thanked God my son was safe and home.

They had a celebration of Tommy's life later that month in August. It was filled to the limit. It was a beautiful testament to his young life. I will never forget the song they played. It was "Forever Young" by Jay-Z. So many people spoke about him and all his antics over the years. One could see he was truly loved and respected. I know Brian wanted to go up and talk about his adventures with Tommy in Europe, but with so many people there, he never had the opportunity. I know that bothered him.

In March of 2012, Brian went skydiving with Tommy's mother in Palmdale. I told him that his Uncle Michael had done that in Houston a few years before he passed. Brian was excited about going and came home all pumped up. He really loved the thrill and the rush of doing it. Brian had no fear whatsoever! It made me think, should I make another bet with him?

In 2012, Brian moved to San Diego after a friend got him a job as a maintenance man at a property management firm. He had several friends who had moved there and already had lined up an apartment with a buddy, Charles. When he was younger, and we took him and Michael to San Diego for weekends, he always said he loved San Diego. Michael had gotten out of the Navy and was working as a union ironworker and had a job offer in Portland, Oregon.

Brian was close, so I knew he would always be back. Michael we would have to go visit, as neither of us had been to Portland. We both always wanted to see that part of the Pacific Northwest.

It was just Jim and I alone again in this big house. Well, not really. Brian did come back a lot to eat us out of house and home. However, with San Diego being so close, we could go there for a few days to visit Brian and find great places to eat. Brian would always ask me to find someplace via Google, especially for his birthday. Sometimes, he would find a nice place for us, and I made sure I always complimented him on his choice.

Jim and I still enjoyed our vacations to Hawaii and our getaway trips to Santa Barbara or San Luis Obispo. Brian would text me if he was coming home, but he wanted us to go visit him a lot.

Brian's roommate, Charles, had a pit bull that I was afraid of. I was always a little cautious around dogs. Brian brought the dog, Casper, home one time, and I was still afraid of him. He was beautiful, all white with such a loving face. Well, he grew on me, and I fell in love with him. Brian would leave him with me when he went out to visit friends. Casper knew who the alpha male was because whenever Brian came back, he went to him. He was OK with me when we were alone watching TV, but when Brian was there, he was all over him. All they want is love and attention and to be fed. You could tell that dog adored Brian, and vice versa. It was a match made in heaven for those two. Brian would take him hiking or to the beach; it seemed Brian took that dog everywhere with him.

I know Brian had a lot of girlfriends, not girlfriends in the romantic sense, but friends. I never delved into his love life but did ask if he was seeing anybody seriously. He would always say the same thing—that he had not met anybody special. Brian was not much of a talker to anybody about those things. I suspect he was deeply hurt at one time and kept a distance so as not to get hurt again. There are just some things you don't share with your mother, no matter how close you are, right?

In the fall of 2012, I was diagnosed with severe arthritis in my knees and back. I started physical therapy, and that helped quite a bit for a time. Jim had a health scare with a tumor on the leg. He lost a lot of weight in a short time and had to have surgery to remove the tumor. Brian and Michael were only a phone call away and promised to come home if need be. I took care of Jim after the surgery, which required changing the bandage and giving him intravenous antibiotics. Shortly, he got better, and all was well again in our world.

One weekend, Brian came home and told me that he had been very low on money and had eaten at a San Diego shelter a few times. He had paid the rent but had nothing left over. My mouth dropped open; I was quite angry and said as much. He said something to me I will never forget, "Mom, there are just some things I have to figure out on my own. I know I can always ask you and Dad, but what happens if you are not here? It was only a few days, and I met some really nice homeless people." What could I say to that? How proud I was of him? YES, I most certainly was. I always knew Brian had a heart of gold and gave to his friends when they needed help.

He came home often when he had the gas money to drive up. He would raid the refrigerator and wash his clothes. Of course he would visit his friends who were in the area.

Around mid-2014, he came home and he was huge, physically. His shoulders and neck were bulging, but mostly his butt was a huge bubble. I was shocked and asked him what he was doing with himself. I knew Jim had spoken to the boys at a young age about the use of steroids. I knew that he was "juicing" and told him so. He said, "Mom, I know what I am doing." What more could I say?

Mostly, I enjoyed hearing him play the piano. It was always comforting to hear him. I had taken lessons and loved playing only what I knew, but Brian was incredible with just sitting there and playing. How does he do that? He never had a lesson, to my knowledge, but he sat there and played like an accomplished pianist. I would see him drawing at the table sometimes, and I would admire the detail. One day, he surprised me and asked me to sit still, and said he would draw me. Well, how could I say no to that? I sat still for about five minutes and was so anxious to see what he had done. It was a drawing of his thumb, as he kept using his thumb to point at me. What a character, for sure!

On New Year's Eve of 2014, Brian told us he was going to see a fight in Vegas and was driving. We told him to be careful and to let us know all was OK. We knew how busy Vegas would be for a huge fight. He did tell me he was taking a girl. I asked him her name, and he said, "Simone." I was over the moon that he was seeing someone. I remember thinking she must be special for him to take her to Vegas.

Whenever Jim and I took off for vacation, we would let Brian know in case he came home. He knew the alarm code to disarm it but always texted me when he was going to the house. He was thoughtful that way and would ask for pictures of where we were. He was particularly interested in our trip to Cape Cod and wanted to see more. I promised him we would take him and his brother if they wanted to go at some point.

Michael got married in a civil ceremony with Quinnia in August of 2015. Neither wanted a wedding but promised to visit us in October. Brian came when they came, and we all had a good time visiting. The three of them would go out and visit Michael and Brian's friends. Quinnia was so sweet, and we were happy for Michael. They had met in basic training in the Navy, so they had known each other a long time.

After they left, it was just Jim and me again, and Thanksgiving was approaching. Brian came home, and I found him outside smoking pot. I took a hit and finished the turkey dinner. It was just us three. I found I was a bit "loaded," and the turkey seemed dry, and I could barely eat. I excused myself and went upstairs to rest. I feel asleep and got up with the munchies. I asked Brian what was in that pot; he laughed and said, "Mom, that was weird smoking pot with one's mother." I laughed and said, "Get over it. I am not dead. I used to smoke it in the 70s." He just laughed.

I told Jim later that night, and he said he had no idea I was even loaded. Oh well, it goes to show you that my husband for over thirty years did not know when I was loaded or not.

With Brian home that Thanksgiving weekend, he mentioned to me that he was boxing as well as doing mixed martial arts. I did not like it one bit and asked him to please be careful. He said that he had gotten himself a long-term disability policy in case anything happened to him. Being a mother, this did not make me feel good at all! I begged him to not do it, but I know my son: he never listens to anybody. I asked Jim to talk to him, and he did and got nowhere. Even he said to me, "You know, Brian. He's always had a mind of his own; he knows what's best for him. He's a grown man and there's nothing we can do but be here for him." I had to agree, but still, I was very uncomfortable with his choice.

At the end of 2015 we decided to sell the house, Jim was getting close to retirement, and we did not want a huge house anymore. We were scheduled to close in early 2016.

Chapter Eight

2016–2017

Brian was serious with Simone and finally told us in early January of 2016. He brought her home to meet us and told us that they were going to move in together. They had known each other for several years, but Brian was not ready at first for a commitment; now he was. Jim and I fell in love with her. Simone was petite, like me, and had the most startling blue-gray eyes. We were so happy for them. Finally, our oldest son was making a life with the love of his life!

Having a big house for that long, we had a lot of "stuff" to get rid of. Brian and Simone came back toward the end of February and rented a truck to move what we were giving them for their home in San Diego. I asked if he wanted the piano, and they said they had no room for it, so I had to arrange storage for it. Brian would get it later down the road when he had a larger place for it. Brian and Simone were so grateful for all the furniture, kitchenware, linens, and other items they wanted. It felt good for Jim and me to be helping them start their lives together. Eventually—marriage, and hopefully grandchildren one day?

What we gave them only made a small dent in all the "stuff" we had collected over the years. We had a garage sale and were left with more than we wanted to take with us.

One morning, I called Brian to ask how things were going. Once in a while a phone call was so much better than a text, which can be impersonal. He was at the Laundromat washing clothes. I was shocked, as I thought he had a washer-dryer at the duplex. He said they did not but was looking at ads for used. I told him he could get brand new appliances at a discount store. I offered to buy him a set, and he was thrilled. He said he would look and let me know the cost. I decided to just send a check instead, and he thanked me profusely when he got it. He and Simone had found a nice set for around $500 and were having it delivered and installed the next day.

Moving day was March 15th, and we moved to a reasonable-sized townhome with a garage, but we still had to rent a storage unit. There are belongings you just are not ready to part with. I caught the flu before the move and was so sick I could barely move. I had zero energy and did the best I could. Thank goodness we had four men help us with the move and a moving van.

We got settled, and I finally got better. In April, Brian asked if we could come to San Diego to meet Simone's mother and stepdad. We were so delighted to do so. Brian had never been this serious before, and we could tell how much they loved each other.

The meeting was perfect. It turned out that Simone had a little half-brother who was only one. We met Gina, Joe, and little Joey. What a truly lovely family; we could not ask for more. It was a lovely dinner and meeting. We took pictures and promised to keep in touch, exchanging phone numbers.

Jim and I were so delighted for our boys. Michael was married, and Brian appeared to be headed that way. We had raised our boys to be adults, and now it was time for us to retire and travel. I wanted to get in touch with my mom's family in England and Australia. Since meeting my Uncle Brian in 1986, we had kept in touch through the years. I wanted to meet my cousin Sharmain. I had another cousin living in Australia; my Uncle Tony's daughter, Dawn, was in Sydney.

That Mother's Day, I received a very nice card from Brian and Simone that made me cry. It was just the sweetest and most heartwarming card Brian had ever sent me. Brian always used the heart instead of "xxx," which was so him. He told me I was the most "amazing" mother ever and to celebrate my day. He also enclosed a gift certificate for a massage, which he knew I loved.

Jim planned to retire in August of 2016, and we planned our trip for the end of August as a retirement present to each of us. We had a travel agent help us with the trip, and both of us decided to go to Fiji first and then Australia and New Zealand since we were so close. I had called my Uncle Brian to let him know we were coming. After all, he was in his eighties, and when would we get to see him if not now? We told the boys we were going and would send pictures along the way. It was a marvelous trip. Meeting my cousins for the first time and seeing my uncle after all those years was really something. He was older, as were Jim and I, but we all got along and loved telling stories about our lives. I fell in love with my cousin Sharmain. She was two years younger than me, and we actually favored each other: same height and build. Jim could not believe it.

Sharmain had arranged a visit for us to see some baby joey's (kangaroos); she was a perfect hostess, as was my uncle. I texted pictures to my sons and daughters-in-law. Simone texted back that she wanted a joey, and I texted back, "Do you know how big they get? Over six feet tall." She texted back, "So?" I really loved this young lady; she was so funny and beautiful.

Fiji was just amazing and relaxing; the people were so friendly and hospitable. It was hard to leave. We loved Australia and all the sites you read about and see on TV. New Zealand was a treat as well. Brian and Michael loved the pictures we sent them. Sometimes, Brian would text me asking where we were and to keep sending the pictures. He texted me that he wanted to go to Australia one day. I texted back, "Perhaps Dad and I can arrange that with all of us one day."

When we got home after the long flight and a rest, we called the boys and asked if they wanted to spend Thanksgiving in Hawaii, the six of us?

They both promised to get back to me after they checked their schedules and spoke to their other halves. Once I got the OK, we booked flights from San Diego for Brian and Simone, and Portland for Michael and Quinnia. We had arranged to meet at the hotel in Waikiki, Jim's and my favorite, the Marriott Waikiki. We sent Brian and Michael money for incidentals so there was no stress getting to and from the airports. We had arranged transportation from the airport in Hawaii to the hotel, figuring that the four of them would possibly be on the same bus in Hawaii.

Suffice to say, it was just so amazing being with my sons in Hawaii again after so many years. This time, each had a partner, and we all went out our first night for dinner and drinks. I had already made a reservation for Thanksgiving dinner at our favorite restaurant, "Roy's" in Waikiki.

Brian and Michael and the girls rented a car one day to go all over the island. Jim and I enjoyed reading and the beach across the street. Since we had seen it all and done it all, we went to relax and veg out.

We had lunch a few times with the family and left them to their own devices at night. We did take them to a magic show, which we all enjoyed before Thanksgiving. I did notice at the beach one day that Brian's back was covered with acne, and his arms and chest were huge. So as not to spoil our trip, I did not say anything to Brian.

Thanksgiving dinner was so special. Brian and Michael ordered lots of appetizers for all of us. Both were funny—they would go overboard with ordering, especially when they knew Mom and Dad were paying. We did not care since we were all together and enjoying the dinner and conversation. Looking back, I am so grateful we had that special time together. We took pictures at the restaurant. We all agreed it was the BEST Thanksgiving ever!

I could not believe that 2017 was upon us. I wondered what would be in store for us. Jim and I decided we both wanted to see Europe. We sat down and went over all the places we wanted to see. After going to Australia and meeting my cousins there, it was time to meet the cousins and see Uncle Tony in England. We planned to leave in early May and return in mid-June. Six weeks seemed like a long time to be gone, but there was so much to see and do. I wanted to be in Paris for my birthday, and Jim agreed we should do it!

I mentioned to Jim that I really wanted to take the family somewhere very special in October or November of 2017. I wanted a tradition of having a really nice vacation with our family before grandchildren arrived and Brian and Michael got too busy. Jim agreed. I had a travel agent research it for me, and I gave him a budget. I then asked the boys where they would want to go if money were no issue. We narrowed it down to the Caribbean. OK, so now where and when? Our travel agent was a jewel; he found a very special place in Grenada, an all-inclusive resort with beachfront rooms for all of us. We then got a date, and Jim and I paid the trip with insurance. It was set for November 2nd to the 10th.

I called my boys and asked them to make sure their passports were up to date. Simone had to find hers, and Brian had to renew his. Michael and Quinnia had theirs.

Before we went to Europe, we visited Brian, Simone, and her family in San Diego. Brian found a nice restaurant for us to meet. We stopped by their duplex beforehand and were amazed at all they had done to fix it up. Brian was proud of the little garden he had of tomatoes, corn, and zucchini. He had Casper visiting and had to take him back home. I was so happy to see him since I fell in love with him. He certainly remembered me and jumped all over me. Such a lovely dog.

A few days before we left for our flight, my cousin Tosh called to say he was coming over at the end of May to LA and wanted to meet us. He and I had a long conversation, and of course I told him we would be in London when he was here. I gave him Brian's phone number and told him that San Diego was a must see on his trip. I then called Brian and explained to him that this was my first cousin but his second, to please take them out to dinner, and I would take care of the expense when I returned. Brian reminded me he owed me some money and not to worry. I did not remember but told him to keep the receipt anyway.

Leaving for six weeks was hard to pack for, since we were starting in Copenhagen and ending in Manchester, UK. We had our itinerary, and we were both very excited. I had spoken to my uncle and gave him the dates we would be in Manchester and when we would be leaving.

During those six weeks, I would text my sons pictures of where we were, and they would text with comments. Brian was especially interested since he had been to most all the places we were visiting. I had always wanted to be in Paris for one of my birthdays, and we were. Copenhagen and Amsterdam were amazingly beautiful, and each offered great places to visit. But Paris was spectacular and more so than my wildest dreams. Both my sons texted me with birthday wishes the morning of my birthday. It was a very special day. It was like being in a completely different world, and we found the French to be very nice and almost everybody spoke English. After that, we took the train to London underneath the English Channel. It was very exciting. We both loved the train system all over Europe, especially first class!

We stayed in London for a few days, and while we were there, my cousin Tosh and his partner, Michelle, were in Los Angeles and drove to San Diego to meet up with Brian and Simone. Brian sent me a picture of them and of course Casper. I was thrilled to see this, and then Tosh sent me one of the same. I was delighted they got to meet each other. Brian texted me, "I paid for dinner as you requested." I asked, "What do I owe you?" He said, "Nothing, you already paid, remember?" Brian was very generous, and I figured I would settle with him when we returned home.

After London, we went to Dublin and Waterford in Ireland and then Edinburgh, Scotland, and then to Manchester to see my Uncle Tony and meet a few of my cousins for the very first time. It was heavenly, and to me six weeks was just not long enough. I mentioned to Jim that I was sad it was coming to an end although happy to go visit our sons for the summer.

We arrived home during the last week of June. Both boys texted to make sure we were home safe and wanted to know when we were coming to visit them. I asked them to let us know since they work—give us some dates and we would make arrangements.

Brian and Simone were available that July, when her grandmother would be visiting. It was just perfect timing, as I really loved Simone's family. We all went out to Roy's restaurant in La Jolla and took pictures and had a lovely time visiting and getting to know each other more.

In August, we flew to Portland to visit Michael and Quinnia. They took us to several great places to eat, since Portland is a "foodie town." Also, we loved going to Voodoo Doughnuts—a must visit in Portland for sure.

On the way back, I told Jim I really wanted to go back to England and see more. He said, "OK, let's do it." I never let moss grow underneath my feet and called my uncle to see how his September was for visitors and also to surprise my cousin Marie for her birthday. I love planning trips and get excited like a little girl on Christmas morning. I had the travel bug now and was anxious to see more of the world; Jim felt the same way.

We arranged to leave just after Labor Day. Brian called and asked if he could use my car for a few days before we left, as his car was in the shop. He mentioned taking Simone and the dogs to Yosemite for four days. Jim and I only had the one car now since we had given Jim's car to Michael and Quinnia, and I had given my car to Brian in 2015. I said "no" since we would be gone for three weeks. He said, "OK, thanks anyway. We will stop to see you on the way. How about dinner?" I said, "Sure, we want to see you and Simone and the dogs."

I was very proud of Brian and Simone because they had adopted a dog from the pound that summer. Brian still picked up Casper at Charles' house to take them all for a hike. Their new dog, Lola was a sweet pit bull, larger than Casper.

Brian and Simone showed up after they visited his great aunt and uncle in North Hollywood around 5:00 p.m. Because they had three dogs with them, we decided to go to a place that had patio dining. It was quite warm outside, and I noticed Brian was very quiet. Simone had shared with me via text that Brian lost a good friend to suicide that weekend. She asked that I not share she told me and to wait for Brian to tell me. He did not say anything at dinner and just remained very quiet. I said, "Honey, is everything all right?" He said, "Yes, all is fine." We finished dinner, and he said they were going to spend the night at Danny's house in Lake Elizabeth and then get an early start the next morning for Yosemite. We would be leaving the next day for London. I asked them to text me when they got to Danny's and also when they arrived at their cabin in Yosemite.

I heard from Simone the next morning when they were on the road to Yosemite. She explained that there was no cell signal on their phones at Danny's, and Brian was driving and wanted me to know all was good.

She said Brian wanted me to text him when we got to London.

I still felt something was off with Brian. I just could not put my finger on it and asked Jim on the way to LAX if he noticed anything with Brian. He did not, so I tried to put it out of my mind. But still, I knew that his friend dying by suicide was not easy, and it broke my heart for his friend and his family.

We had the opportunity to meet my cousin Tosh and his partner, Michelle, in London a few times before we headed to see his dad, my uncle. We had plenty of time to explore the city again, and this time we were right by the London Eye. I took so many photos and sent them to my boys and girls. Jim and I loved the walks we took around the city. We planned to go to Manchester on the train for a week, and then we booked a nice hotel in the country outside of South Hampton. We would end up back in London for four days before our flight back home.

When we got to Manchester, I received a text from Brian asking if he could borrow some money; he had hurt his back and needed some time off work. I texted him back, "Sure, how much?" He asked for $1,500 and if I could go through Venmo. I said Chase Bank would be easier for me. So I did it, and the next morning he texted to ask if we could talk. I knew the time change was eight hours, so I called, and I was shocked to hear how fast he was talking. He seemed almost manic to me. He begged me to cancel the Chase and to do the wire through Venmo. He did not have an account with Chase, and he just could not figure out how to get the money with his bank.

I let him talk, and then he told me about the suicide of his friend Drew. He told me he was having a hard time dealing with his friend doing that. I asked him how it happened, and he said, "He took a gun to his chest while Rachael was in the kitchen cooking dinner." I could hear he was devastated and told him I was so very sorry. He then said he had hurt his back at the gym and needed some rest.

I wired the money to him via Venmo, and shortly after that I received a beautiful text, thanking me and saying I was "the BEST Mother EVER!" He said, "Enjoy the rest of your trip, and sorry for bothering you." I never felt my boys were a bother in any shape or form. I loved being a mother, and as long as I was alive, I wanted to be able to help them in any way I could.

We stayed with my uncle, and I surprised my cousin Marie for her birthday. It was so very lovely being with my mother's family and being in the country of her birth. After we left my uncle, we took the train to South Hampton and got to our hotel in the country. It was just marvelous and so very relaxing. We hired a driver one day to take us to Stonehenge. Neither of us felt comfortable driving on the "wrong side of the road."

It was a cold and rainy day at Stonehenge. I am so glad Jim convinced me to get some good shoes that were waterproof in Portland at our favorite Columbia store. After Stonehenge, we stopped in Salisbury and had a great lunch at a local pub with our driver. We walked around for a bit before we headed back.

The next day, we took the train to Bath. On the train, I received a text from Simone's mother, Gina, asking if we were still abroad. I knew something was up but did not feel it was an emergency and texted back that we would be home the following week. She texted me back with the thumbs-up sign.

Bath was so magical. We took a tour of the Roman baths and had high tea at the restaurant. Jim and I were amazed at the history and the lovely gardens and the cleanliness of the city. I felt as if I had been there before, perhaps a past life?

The last part of our trip was back to London to spend four days with my cousin Tosh and partner, Michelle. They offered for us to stay with them for the last days. It would be fun living like a local in London in an area close to Kensington. We were both excited and took the train to London, enjoying the countryside along the route.

Once there, we took a taxi to Tosh and Michelle's flat and met them. It was a lovely flat: three stories with steps up to the living room and kitchen and with the bedrooms and bath upstairs. We were so happy to see how locals live in a huge city like London. The Tube was literally down the street from where they lived with restaurants and myriad tea and coffee shops.

We all went to dinner that night at an Italian restaurant within walking distance. The next day they both worked, so they offered to show us how to use the Tube. We bought an Oyster card, and since we had used the subway in Paris, we both learned pretty quickly. We had the flat to ourselves and walked around and found a place for lunch and groceries. In the meantime, I received a call from Simone to please call her anytime, no matter the time. I was upset and mentioned it to Jim. We agreed we would call when we got back to the flat. My stomach was flip-flopping as I could not imagine what was going on—was my Brian hurt? I did not have a good feeling.

We called Simone as soon as we got back to the flat. It was still early in San Diego, and she was crying. She told us that Brian had been acting very strange lately and told her he needed time apart since the death of his friend Drew. She was distraught because he had not been working and was using a lot of pot and was taking steroids. She just spilled it all out and told us she was concerned for him. Even his work had called her and told her he was acting strange and saying weird things. She mentioned that he had received a blow to the head while boxing at the gym several days ago. He had come home and complained about a headache and lay down and slept for quite some time. I was really concerned now that he had a concussion and with smoking pot and using steroids he was exacerbating the situation. We were leaving later the next day, and I was a wreck. She asked us not to tell Brian and that if we could call him just to see what our thoughts were, she would feel so much better.

I called Brian, and he answered and asked why I was calling. I just said I wanted to hear his voice and see how he was doing. He then said, "I know Simone put you up to this, Mommy." I was shocked. Brian never called me "Mommy"—it was always "Mom." Now I was really concerned. Jim got on the phone to talk to him, and Brian hung up on his father. So unlike him. Jim called back, and Brian said he did not want to talk to us because he knew we were calling on behalf of the FBI and CIA, and we were in cahoots with the people who were following him. Oh boy, my baby was really going off the deep end. What was going on?

He started texting really strange stuff. I can't even imagine what was going on in his head. I was totally heartbroken and so very upset that we were eight thousand miles away and would not be home until really late the next night. The texts went on for several hours; they were worse and worse, with him saying "the man in ceiling was talking to him." I was going out of my mind with worry and concern. Jim said to call Simone and tell her to send a friend over to check on him. That's what I did. I spoke to her and said he sounds delusional and very paranoid. I asked if she would please call Charles and ask him to check on him. She promised she would. I told her we were going out, as it was our last night, and we'd be home late the next night. I asked her to call me tomorrow. We agreed to speak first thing in the morning or on the way to the airport.

When Tosh and Michelle got home from their jobs, we went to a fabulous Indian restaurant. I was sick to my stomach and barely ate. I just wanted to be with my son and see what was happening to him. I was very sad but tried not to show it. I could not imagine what was going on with my poor baby. What happened?

We went back to pack for the next day and fly home. It had been such a great trip, but now it was time to get back to reality and what our son was going through.

I left my phone on all night in case Simone called, and she did. It was 6:00 a.m. London time, so it had to be ten at night in San Diego. She was crying and said that Brian was incarcerated. I was not sure I heard her and asked again what happened. Jim and I were listening together, and Jim took my hand while Simone told us what she knew: "Brian was arrested for vandalizing five cars in the neighborhood. He thought he was being watched by the Secret Service. When the police came, he went willingly with no fight. He is in the San Diego County jail."

I was crying and so very upset. Simone was overwhelmed with the whole situation and was staying with her mother. We could not do anything until we got back to the States later that night.

We arranged to speak to her later and told her to get some rest. We told her we loved her and that we would be home soon to assess the situation.

Needless to say, after we said our goodbyes to Tosh and Michelle and got into the car taking us to the airport, I was totally depressed. I could not help but think of what my son was going through. Was he being mistreated? Why had he vandalized those cars? What the heck was going on?

At Heathrow, our phone started ringing with a call from

San Diego. When I accepted it, it was the jail, but I could not accept Brian's call due to his needing money on his account. I would have to call an 800 number and provide a credit card for Brian to place calls outside the jail.

I was so upset that I could not talk to my son. He may have forgotten in his delusional and paranoid state that we were on our way back from London. My heart was bleeding for him. Jim got on the phone at a coffee shop in the middle of the airport to try unsuccessfully to get Brian some credit for phone calls. I texted Simone to ask her if she went to see him to please let him know what we had to do for him to place calls. We would add her number as well so he could call out to either of us.

The flight from London to Los Angeles was the longest flight of my life. Although it was only ten hours, I was antsy and could not sleep, read, or watch a movie. My mind would not shut off; all I could envision was what my son was going through. He'd never been in jail before. I just could not imagine what had happened to him and how he was being treated. My heart was so heavy.

We finally landed; it seemed like days since we left London. I could not wait to get home, sleep, and get to San Diego as soon as possible.

The next day was Friday, September 29th. We were both exhausted, and I managed to sleep in. Once awake, all I could think about was my Brian. I got up, unpacked, washed clothes, and tried again to get a credit card for Brian to make calls to us and Simone. I also looked Brian up on the San Diego Central Jail website. It was so hard to find him and took quite a bit of time. When I did, the site said he was not allowed visitors. However, I did get Brian credits for his calls to us.

I called Simone and found out that his arraignment date was Monday, October 2nd. I told her we would be there so we could see him. We would drive down on Sunday to meet her and her mother if we could arrange where to meet.

Jim got up, and I told him what was happening. He was very upset but was thankful we had a few days to rest before leaving on Sunday for San Diego. Jim had not slept on the plane either.

All we could do was wait for Brian to call us. I found a hotel for us on Sunday night close by the courthouse so we could walk there on Monday morning. Never having been to an arraignment before, neither of us knew what to expect.

We got into San Diego for a late lunch with Simone; her mother, Gina; and little Joey. We would check into our hotel after we met up with them to find out what happened with Brian.

What Simone told us was eye-opening. Jim and I just sat there and let her tell us all that had transpired with our son.

She told us he had been taking steroids and smoking a lot of pot. He was distraught over the loss of Drew and told her he was grieving and needed a week apart. She did mention that on or about September 20th he had come home and complained about being hit on the head during boxing. He went to sleep and got up hours later. His work noticed he was talking and acting strangely and called her to tell her this. She felt he had pretty much kicked her out of the duplex they shared and which she paid half the rent for.

All we could do was listen and see what we could do to help her. It was already the first of October, and rent was due. We asked Simone what she wanted to do. She told us she could not go back to the duplex after what Brian had done to the cars. We agreed and offered to help her monetarily to find a place and move.

We said our goodbyes and told Simone we would let her know what happened the next day in court. We checked into our hotel, walked to find the courthouse, ate dinner, and then went back. All the while, my brain was on overload. We could not even see Brian or talk to him prior to the hearing. What in the heck was happening to our smart, generous, kind-hearted son? Why in the world was he self-medicating? Taking steroids and smoking pot when he of all people knew the danger of steroids in particular? Jim and I were dumbfounded. All we could do was be there for him and support him as parents do for their children.

We got to the courthouse in plenty of time. Of course, we had to wait for other cases to be heard and hopefully meet with a public defender at some point, perhaps after the hearing? We did not know the process, but we sure were going to learn. After a few hours, Brian's name was finally called, and there was our son. He looked good—lean and tanned. He stood much taller than the public defender and seemed to be OK physically. When the judge asked how he pleaded, he started saying, "I am guilty." The judge looked at him and asked if family were there, and we raised our hands. Brian then looked over and saw us. The public defender was trying to talk to Brian and tell him he had to plead "not guilty," but he would not listen. He then said, "My mother always said I should be a lawyer, so now I am going to defend myself." The judge stepped in and said, "Brian, this is only an arraignment, not a trial; you need to plead 'not guilty' so we can move on. Your parents are here, so please don't make this harder on them. Do what the public defender tells you." Bless the judge—she could see how upset we were and so wanted to tell Brian to do what needed to be done for the time being. Finally he relented, and the public defender said, "Not guilty," and then he asked for a drop in bail, which was posted at $50,000. The prosecuting attorney denied a reduction. That was that for now. Brian was led away by the deputies.

Jim and I went into the hall to meet with the public defender. He was a nice guy and said that he was just there to be on the record and that a public defender would be assigned to Brian within a few days. He gave us the phone number to call in a few days and offered his best to us and Brian.

Jim and I had a lot to discuss and needed to talk to Brian. But since he was not allowed visitors, all we could do was wait for his call.

Naturally, I wanted to bail him out, but Jim had a good response to that. If we did, and Brian was delusional and paranoid, what would happen to him? He needed treatment and help desperately. All we could do was wait to find out who would be assigned as his public defender so we could talk to him or her.

I called Simone and her mother and told them the news about what happened in court. My heart was aching, but it was also aching for Simone. She did not deserve this. Jim and I promised we would do all we could to help her.

We also had to call our Michael and tell him what his brother was going through. We knew Michael was on a big job in Portland and had to wait until he got off work. We had been texting him with an update on our trip and when we arrived home but did not want to tell him about his brother until we could have a conversation.

We drove back home and waited for Brian to call us when he could. Simone could not see him either; none of us could. Now, all we could do was play the waiting game.

It was not easy telling Michael what was going on with his brother. He was sad and upset to hear his brother was in jail. What more could we say? He wanted to be kept posted. We promised we would.

Finally, later that week, I received a call from my son at 9:30 a.m. In the interim, we had called and received the name of his public defender and left a message. I was elated as I accepted Brian's call. When he spoke, he was manic, going off in a thousand directions. It was my son, sounded like him, but it was not my Brian. He was so delusional and told me his version of what happened. My heart was already broken and bleeding, but now the wound was wide open. He was so out of it and told me things I knew were not true. I knew who the president of our country was and the vice president; he had it mixed up and said he was being followed by the Secret Service because of what he posted on the internet. He mentioned algorithms and such and went off. All I could do was listen and try to get a word in when I could. "How are you being treated?" I asked. He went off on that and said he was in the psych ward and "they" were trying to poison him with medication, which he refused to take. He went off on a tirade until he had to go; we only got twenty minutes or so. He said he would call again when he could.

Jim was still in bed, and I went upstairs, crying. I told him what Brian said, and all he could do was hold me. I just could not imagine what was going on with my poor baby. How did he get this way? Was it the steroids, pot, hit on the head? What in the hell was going on with our son?

Brian always seemed to have confidence, whereas Michael did not. As I mentioned earlier, they got along great. They both had their own unique personalities and both were extremely loving and kind. Michael had behavioral issues early on and was doing great now. Was our Brian going through what Michael went through but in his thirties? I just could not fathom. Our world as we knew it was now shattered into a million pieces.

I was trying to hold it together while my son was going through his journey in a jail cell. I just could not think of anything else but my son.

He called most mornings when he could around 9:30 a.m. This was great for me, since I was up. We would speak, but he was so out of it. He complained about the food and asked if I could get something to him. He mentioned the commissary at the jail; if I ordered in the morning, it would be delivered to him that evening. I did manage to get into the jail website and order some food. He wanted paper, pencils, and envelopes as well. No problem. I found that I could email him, and it would be delivered the next day.

Brian started sending letters to us and calling Simone as well. At this point, I felt I needed to see my psychologist to help me understand what Brian was going through.

We finally got the name of Brian's public defender, a woman. Jim and I spoke to her, and she seemed really nice. We both told her we were very concerned about our son being delusional and very paranoid. I asked if she could get an MRI on him since he had had a hit on the head September 20th, according to his girlfriend. She said I would have to speak to the medical unit at the jail.

We found out his next court date was October 12th. We asked if we needed to be there, and the public defender said it was not necessary. Simone said she would go and call us with the details.

To this day, I am so sorry I did not go to that court date. Brian had only met with the public defender a few days prior to the court appearance and told his story to her. At the hearing, according to Simone, she went in front of the judge and said that Brian needed psychological examination to determine if he was able to stand trial. The judge gave a date of November 28, 2019 for the court-appointed psych evaluation, with a return to court on December 18, 2019. According to Simone, Brian was furious in court and told the public defender that she "screwed him." This meant that Brian had to stay in jail another two-and-a-half months! I was furious too!

Yes, Brian needed help but not to be in jail for this long for a psych evaluation. I needed to call some criminal attorneys. I had no faith in the public defender now. I did call her and had to leave a message. When we did speak, I was very curt with her, asking why she did not ask the judge for a sooner evaluation? I let her know that this was unacceptable to me, a mother, for my son to sit in jail for that long for vandalism charges, and his being in a delusional and paranoid state. He needed medical help, not jail.

I checked Google and Yelp to find some good attorneys in downtown San Diego. Several called me back, and Jim, Simone, and I arranged to meet with one the following week.

I gave Simone the address to meet us, and we all went in to see the attorney. First of all, he had a conflict of interest with the public defender that was working Brian's case. His wife and she were really good friends. However, he did say it would be in our interest to obtain our own psychological evaluation for Brian. He gave us a few names and numbers and wished us luck. We did put him on retainer in case we had any more questions or concerns.

During this time, I was calling the medical department of the jail. I was trying to get as much information on Brian as to his mental state.

There were some wonderful nurses, and I found out that labs and blood had been taken upon his booking. Brian had already signed a release that I could speak to them, and they could give me information. I also got the name of his psychiatrist. Bingo, I was making progress. I left him a message for him to call me.

Our family vacation to Grenada was coming up fast, and of course Brian was incarcerated and could not go. I had to cancel his and Simone's tickets which saddened me. Brian had texted us while we were in England that he planned to propose to Simone as soon as he hit the beach at the resort. Jim and I were delighted and so happy we would be there to witness the proposal.

During this time, our Michael's wife was having some medical issues as well. She was in the hospital, and Michael did not think they could go to Grenada as well. He was worried and asked if I had obtained insurance for the trip. I told him not to worry—I had insurance—just to take care of his wife and keep me posted. He was very concerned for his brother and wanted me to have Brian call him when he could.

Brian's psychiatrist, Dr. Roman (name has been changed), called me later the next evening. Bless him; what a wonderful man. He did say he needed a release signed from Brian before he could talk to me. He would be seeing Brian the next day and promised to call me after Brian signed the release.

True to his word, Dr. Roman called me. We spoke about Brian's delusions and paranoia. He asked me if he had ever exhibited this kind of behavior before. I asked him if Brian told him about the steroids and pot; he said yes, he had. I asked how all the blood tests were, and he said there weren't any signs of drugs in his system. I told him about the hit on the head and that he had slept afterward, according to Simone. He did tell me a brain tumor could mirror psychotic behavior and that he would have the medical doctor order a MRI. He did mention that Brian would not take any medications whatsoever; he did not trust anybody.

At this point, Brian was in a segregated unit in the jail, not the general population. During his booking on September 27, he had told the officer in charge of booking him that he was suicidal. The officer also deemed he was clearly delusional. Dr. Roman mentioned he would try and get Brian on the psych ward as soon as a bed became available.

While all this was going on, Simone wanted to get another apartment. Now, we had to go move Brian's belongings out and help Simone monetarily to move. So much was happening it made my head spin.

I also had to take care of the trip and let our travel agent know what we were dealing with. There was no problem with Michael because we could get proof that Quinnia was in the hospital. Being in jail was not a valid excuse to cancel a trip, according to the insurance. I asked my agent to cancel, and we would deal with the insurance later. However, there were six of us who were supposed to go. What could we say to get our money back? Jim and I decided that we should go and let the kids know we would all go another time.

My psychologist, Dr. Dunn, felt Jim and I should go and not worry about Brian; he was being taken care of medically. After speaking to Dr. Roman, I did feel somewhat OK that my son was being taken care of. Brian was also telling us he was a political prisoner—another wound in my already broken heart for my son.

We finally got a call from the psychologist that the attorney referred us to, Dr. Jacobs (name has been changed). I cannot forget, as it was Halloween and she had to take her children trick or treating. She really sounded wonderful and promised she would see Brian before the court-appointed evaluator. She gave us her fee, we agreed, and I gave her a credit card. I finally felt I could breathe.

Simone found a nice apartment in Hillcrest; we gave her the deposit. We called their landlord and because Brian was in jail, she would allow them to move out by the end of October. She was very sorry about Brian and would send his deposit to me so I could deposit it in his account.

We went back to San Diego to help Simone pack and got to see Brian. He was finally able to have visitors, and it would be our first time having face-to-face conversation since we saw him and Simone before we left for England.

We had so much to learn about our jail system. Visitations were scheduled online only. You had to arrive forty-five minutes prior to your visit with an inmate and have your identification to show the clerk. So, you had forty-five minutes to wait to see them. The jail in San Diego is a high-rise and looked fairly new.

Brian looked good! He was my handsome son, and I was just so very sorry to see him behind glass and using a phone to talk. He sounded like my son, but his mind was not there. He was saying things like he was a billionaire and owned all the buildings in downtown San Diego. He was a political prisoner because he knew what was going on in this country. That is why he was being followed and why they wanted him out of the way. It was always "they." I tried to understand, but like Jim said, he was in his own world. It was so very sad and heartbreaking to see my son this way. I told Brian that I knew about the steroids, and he said he had not been taking any since a week before he was locked up. He was talking so fast, my head was spinning. He spoke to his dad for a bit, and then it was time to go. I told him I wished I could hug him. He did tell me it was not so bad there; they gave you three meals a day and with what I was sending to him, he was making do.

I started going to see him very early Sunday mornings—there was no traffic from our house to San Diego, and it only took me a little over two hours. In the meantime, he was sending letters and calling. I had told him we hired a psychologist to visit him and give him an evaluation of our own. I told him to be up front with her and to let us know when she came and that it was supposed to be before the court-appointed one.

October was a very long month with all we had going on: back and forth to San Diego, helping Simone move, dealing with the trip cancellation for four people, and calling the jail to speak to the nurses about how our son was doing. We were to leave for Grenada on November 2nd for seven nights. As much as I wanted to go when I booked the trip, I now no longer wanted to go. This was supposed to be a family vacation. Brian was in jail and Quinnia was out of the hospital but could not travel due to doctor's orders.

I let Brian know that we were going, and he gave us his blessing. He said he was fine and not to worry. Sometimes, he sounded like himself, until he would go off on a tirade again about being a political prisoner.

Jim and I left for Miami to catch our connecting flight to Grenada. It was a very long day but worth it when we arrived at the resort. I only wished my family was with us. It was just beautiful! The ocean was an aquamarine color, sparkling, and with a clean smell. No smog here on this tiny island in the Caribbean Sea and Atlantic Ocean. Our room had the most magnificent view, which the boys would have had as well. The sunset was remarkable—all the colors you can imagine in a sunset. I was happy to be there, but a sadness overtook me, and Jim did his best to cheer me up.

Looking back, the week seemed to last forever. We were busy all day swimming in the warm water, taking boat rides, snorkeling, and touring the island. We met some wonderful people from New Hampshire and Canada, and enjoyed the entertainment. The food was absolutely delicious—lots of fish, which we both love. Both of us commented several times how much Brian, Simone, Michael, and Quinnia would love it there.

Dr. Roman, the jail psychiatrist, did call me late one night while we were in Grenada to give me a report on Brian. He was still refusing medications and seemed more agitated. The medical doctor had ordered a CT scan, not an MRI. The scan was on the schedule, and he would let me know when it would occur. I then told him Jim and I would pay for an MRI. He did say they were trying to move Brian to the general population, and Brian had a fit. He wanted to be segregated and seemed to do well there. However, he was still on the medical floor and getting counseling and medical attention. He was drawing a lot and reading. I told Dr. Roman that we would be back in a few days, and I would get there to see Brian.

My heart was so heavy thinking of my Brian. I ached all over and felt like I betrayed him by taking a vacation while he was in jail. So many thoughts in my head were racing around like a wildfire. I believe only a mother could understand. How I wish my mom was here so I could talk to her. She always had the best advice, and I tried so much to be like her with my boys. I could only pray to God to keep Brian safe and help him heal.

When we returned home, I called the nursing station to see how Brian was and scheduled a visit. I noticed he could have visits a few times a week instead of only one day. I called Simone to see if she had gone to see him, and she had. She was also receiving letters from him and seemed OK. Bless her heart. She had moved to her apartment and seemed happy there but still wanted Brian with her. Most of his belongings were there; I took some things to store for him. My son had a lot of shoes and clothes. His car was an issue, as it was parked on the street and needed to be moved every so often. I mentioned to Simone that if it became a problem, we would bring it to our house. She agreed, but first we needed to discuss it with Brian.

Brian's CT scan was scheduled and still had not been done. I was upset and left a message for Dr. Roman.

I went to see Brian on Sunday, since it was easy with the traffic, and I could return home that afternoon. Brian was tired, as they had to wake him. He was quite agitated and told me they had woken him early to take him for the CT scan but left him in a room for two hours. He was then taken back to his cell with no explanation except it was cancelled. He was still delusional and then asked if I had a copy of *People* magazine, as he was named "The most influential person of the year." I was taken aback and asked him, "Why?" He said, "You don't know?" I said, "No, honey, I don't. I have not seen the magazine, as we just returned from Grenada, remember?" He then floored me with his answer, "I solved the theory of everything." He was so proud of himself. I wanted to cry but held it until I left. He said he sent me his theory and to take care of it for him. He then asked for me to start sending some books to him. He wanted to read more and wanted to learn Chinese, Russian, and Japanese. I told him I would see what I could do.

I literally cried all the way home. It was blinding, but I did not want to stop. I just wanted to get home and talk to Jim about what our son was going through.

Jim was always supportive. He let me vent and talk about what Brian was going through. Jim knew Brian and I were very close. I really think it was harder for Jim to see Brian in jail, and he could not do it. I, on the other hand, needed to see him and be there for him. He called my cell and Simone's whenever he could. Brian and I went through a lot before he came into this world; we were both in distress, and according to Jim, we both could have died in another era.

On Monday, after my visit with Brian, I called the nursing station about why the CT scan was cancelled. I was told there was an emergency within the department and all deputies were needed. That is why Brian was left in a room for over two hours. It was rescheduled, and they would let me know when. I told the lovely nurse that Jim and I would pay for an MRI rather than a CT scan. She said she would relay the message.

Dr. Jacobs still had not been to see Brian, so I left her a message and was texted back that she would see him soon and promised it would be before the court-appointed psych.

Brian finally had the CT scan, not an MRI, and it was declared normal. All his blood work came back and was all good. So, what was going on? If no steroids were in his system, why was he delusional and paranoid? My psychologist, Dr. Dunn, said it was the pot and told me stories about some of his patients going paranoid and delusional with constant smoking.

During the month of November, I was back and forth to San Diego. I loved seeing Brian and always felt he looked good. He was in good shape; he told me he was exercising and writing a lot besides reading. He received the books I sent him and all the food. He seemed in good spirits. Thanksgiving was approaching, and I really was angry about his being there for the holiday. Thanksgiving was my favorite holiday. How could I enjoy it with my son in there?

Simone and I had agreed to meet together at the jail to visit Brian the Monday prior to Thanksgiving. Afterward, I would meet her and her family for an early dinner at Mimi's Cafe. I was looking forward to seeing Gina, Joe, and little Joey.

Simone and I met for an iced tea before going up to see Brian. She seemed in good spirits and was looking forward to seeing him. I agreed to give her more time after I spoke with him for a few minutes.

Brian seemed very manic and was talking very rapidly. He was also talking about conspiracy theories. After we spoke, Simone got on the phone, and I moved down to the far end. I could hear Brian yelling but could not understand what he was saying. After what seemed like fifteen minutes, Simone started banging the phone and yelled at Brian. I got up and asked what was going on? Brian told Simone he was in love with someone else and was breaking up with her. What? I got on the phone to Brian and said, "She has been here for you during this whole time. Has this other person you claim to love been to see you? Called you? What is going on?" Brian just looked at me, and I hung up. Simone had already left the floor and was on the elevator on the way down.

I caught up with her and told her she had to understand he was sick. She was crying, and I was trying to calm her down. I did not want her driving home in this state. I hugged her and told her to please try and see it this way: Brian is very ill right now. He is delusional and thinks he loves someone else. We were on the street corner and people were looking at us. She left, and I got into my car and immediately called her mother. I told Gina what had happened. She thanked me and told me she would talk to Simone.

I called Michael on the way to my hotel and told him what had happened. I remember we were talking as I drove, and he listened to me. Gina was trying to get ahold of me, but I was on the phone with my Michael. I needed to hear his words and what he was thinking about the incident with his brother and Simone.

Michael had a way of calming me down. After all the therapy he had had through the years with his issues, he really understood. We spoke all the way while I was driving to my hotel. I thanked him and then called Jim. Jim always listened and was so sorry for the incident and told me to try and enjoy the dinner with Simone and her family.

I got to the hotel to lie down for a bit. I was emotionally exhausted and cried myself to sleep. When I awoke after only an hour, there was a message from my sister Diane. I listened to it and found out my baby sister Cindy had passed away that morning. OK, anything else? Why was all this going on in my life and around me? God, please, how much more was I supposed to take? It was then that I heard my mother's voice, "God only gives you what you can handle." I guess God knew I could handle this and move on. All part of life's journey.

I called Diane to find out what happened. Cindy left two sons and had been living with my sister Gail. It was an apparent overdose. She had been on heroin for years and was skin and bones. It broke my heart, thinking of her as my baby sister who I used to protect and take care of. I called both my nephews and offered my condolences and told them to call me if they needed anything.

I don't remember if I called Gina and Simone or if they called me. I just knew I could not go out to eat and be in anybody's company right now. I was just overwhelmed and needed to be alone. I called Jim and told him, and he was so calming. I asked him if I should check out and come home. He said, "Stay the night. Get some rest. You are in no condition to drive home right now." As always, he was right.

I did not hear from Brian for several days, but I did receive a letter. He did not apologize but said it was not a good visit. He went on a rant about his situation and told me he was OK and would survive all this.

Thanksgiving was upon us and no call from Brian. I was sad that he was spending his holiday in jail but knew he was safe. I was hoping he would call that weekend; either way I would go see him on Sunday morning.

I left very early on Sunday and got there in plenty of time to check in and get some coffee. Our visit was at 9:30 a.m., and I was anxious to see him after our last visit.

I was amazed: he was awake and alert. He told me the Thanksgiving meal was the best he had there since he was booked. I was elated and asked him to tell me all about it. He asked me if I received his letter, and I said I had. He said, "Which one?" I told him about his saying it was a bad visit with Simone and me. He said, "No, I sent you my meditations and reflections for Thanksgiving." I told him I had not received it yet but would let him know. He did explain why he did not call over the holiday; the jail was short staffed and they hardly left their cells except to eat. He was sorry he did not call. I told him that explained it.

I then asked, "Has anyone come to visit, such as the psychologist we hired or the court-appointed one?" He replied, "No, I've seen nobody but you and Simone."

After our visit, I made a note to call Dr. Jacobs and see what was going on. We had already paid her, and she promised she would see him prior to November 18th. I also needed to call the medical staff to see if the court-appointed one had indeed come to see him. Maybe Brian was mistaken? Although he was very manic, delusional, and paranoid, he was not so out of it to know if someone besides me or Simone came to visit.

On Monday, I called the nursing staff to see if anyone had seen Brian. I was told that nobody outside of the medical staff had. I called Dr. Jacobs and left her a message explaining she had still not seen Brian. We wanted the independent evaluation before Brian spoke to the court-appointed evaluator. She texted me back that she would go that week.

In the meantime, my sessions with Dr. Dunn were very helpful in dealing with Brian. I was not to challenge Brian but ask questions, interact with him by being supportive and listening. Most importantly, I was not to go along with his delusions. My son had a mental disorder, and he needed help desperately. Since he had let his insurance lapse, the medical unit at the jail was taking care of him. I still tried talking to him about taking medication. He refused, as he still thought he was being poisoned.

The Tuesday after Thanksgiving, I received his meditations and reflections in the mail. I cried as I read it. He certainly knew his grandparents, his dad, brother, and me. He wrote so eloquently and from the heart. I had to share:

My Meditations & Reflections

Thanksgiving 2017

By Brian Dubrasky

From my grandma Mimi, I learned that unconditional love pays for itself in full. That kindness and tenderness foster extreme grace and gratitude.

From my grandma Nana, I learned that it's better to face your fears and recognize the past atrocities that occurred so that you force yourself to face the truth. I also gained a reinforced sense of unconditional love from the kindness and generosity she gave to her entire family.

From my Grandpa Jack, I learned that strong men can be broken, but even when you are broken you can still find strength and solitude and peace in your scarred and hardened state. He never appeared normal or sane to me but never was he in anyway evil nor mad nor crazy, just neutral and calm like a monk determined to sit quietly and mediate for the rest of his days.

From my Grandfather George, I learned that tough love is still real love. I learned that it is better to be strong rather than weak because it is better to fight and die rather than run and live as a coward. To die on your feet rather than live on your knees—to always shine with pride and honor so you avoid death which always supersedes dishonor. I also learned that one can appear angry and mean but also show extreme generosity, like how he always gave everything to his family, first without ever asking anything in return, except to always show respect and to learn to reciprocate first with gratitude and thus to always give more than you take out which is the core definition of generosity.

From my Mother, I inherently received all the love that a mother could possibly give and I learned the value of hard work and that a woman can be even stronger than a man. She always ran the house and wore the proverbial pants and thus created a pleasurably harmonious environment, giving me and my brother a childhood that was absolutely magical and carefree. I grew up with a sense of Mystism and wonder that can only be categorized as "Perfect" to me.

From my Father, I learned that a strong man could also be smart and could even show the grace and kindness and love that boys usually only expect from their mothers. He gave me every tool he could give, just like he picked me up and held me above his head every time I wanted to fly high in the sky. All I had to say was "Daddy, pick up Brian," as I'm so fondly reminded of. He always did everything in his power to foster the mind above all to thus create a strong body with a proud heart. So learned was he, always passed down to us all the worldly knowledge even before we knew how to ask. He always told us the real truth of the past captured from the objectivity that he discovered from the many pages of history that he seared endlessly for. It was his stories that inspired me the most. I learned the value of analogy, syllogism, alliteration, and of course good satire and humor before I even knew what any of those words meant.

From my brother Michael, I learned how to see myself in others. I learned that everyone has different strengths and weaknesses. I was a physically "slow developer" while his body grew up bigger and faster than mine. We hardly ever fought as kids instead we became best friends. I learned not to envy him and the fact that he was already bigger and taller than me in grade school. I learned by watching him, that defiance can have bitter results and that being cunning and sly isn't the same as being smart. Still in the end it's not how you start but how you finish. And, if we were to call this day the end we could say he finished as a good husband and a journey man iron worker who also served this country well as an enlisted man in the Navy.

I was so very proud of him, and I told him when he called that my heart was bursting with pride! He was happy that I had received the letter. He wanted all of us to know how much he loved us. Even though he was holed up in jail, he still knew that he had a loving family. Jim and I both felt Brian was letting us know that we did right; we gave him all the opportunities in life to grow and be a great man. To be told I was "perfect" as a mother was the highest compliment. Jim was also honored as well as Michael. It filled my heart with such joy and gratitude!

At the end of the week, I called the nursing staff again and found out that the court-appointed psychologist had met with Brian on November 28. The one we hired still had not gone to see our son. I was getting quite agitated with her, as we had specifically asked that she go before Thanksgiving. I called her again and was told she would go that Friday.

Didn't I have enough stress to not need more from someone you hire to do a job and who has been paid for almost a month? What kind of person does that? In hindsight, I should have fired her, but I continued on because of my love for Brian.

Brian called over the weekend, and we had a good talk. He was still out of it but appeared to not be as manic and was drawing a lot. He asked for more books to read and more money on his account. I always sent him more than he asked for and plenty of food. I know Brian missed the foods he loved, sushi being one of them. He had now been in there two months, and we still had to go to court on December 18 to see what the court-appointed psychologist recommended. Still, ours had not shown up.

Dr. Roman called and gave me an update. Brian was a bit calmer and not as manic but still refusing medication. He also told me Brian was writing and drawing a lot; his cell had a lot of pictures of images he had drawn. Dr. Roman even mentioned how talented Brian was. Although still delusional and paranoid, Brian seemed to be coming around. He kept a clean cell, and his person was clean. That was good news.

December was here, and it was only eighteen days to go before we had to go back to court. I asked Brian what he wanted to do when he got out. He told me he had plenty of places to go and since he owned so many buildings, he would find something. This was hard to swallow. I asked about Simone, and he was evasive. I think he was confused and really did not know what he wanted when he got out. Again, I mentioned taking medication, and he refused.

Finally, after way too many calls asking when she was going, Dr. Jacobs finally saw Brian on December 6th. She called us later that afternoon and spoke to Jim and me on my speaker phone. What she said was quite astounding:

"I spent three hours with your son, and he is one cool dude. He is smart, very talented, and knows right from wrong. He and I had a great conversation about books, and I recommended some to him. I would say he is very competent to stand trial. I did not know that Pence is president of the US. Did you?" I sucked in my breath and did not say anything until she was done. I was absolutely furious with her and felt it was money that was flushed down the toilet. She proceeded to say, "I told Brian to get his hair cut and to take the medication his doctor is prescribing. I also told him he should make a plea with the DA." As if she had some power over our son…who in the hell did she think she was?

She then asked why I was upset over her agreeing with his delusions, and I told her what my own psychologist said. Her answer was, "I wanted to make friends with him and felt this was the best course of action." Wow! She actually received a license as a psychologist?

I could not wait to tell Dr. Dunn and obtain his thoughts on her evaluation.

Brian called the next day and told me Dr. Jacobs had met him. He liked her and told me she was really cool and that she agreed with him that Pence was president. Of course my son liked her, she had agreed with his delusions. I asked him about how long she spent with him, and he said, "Funny you should ask, I saw the time when I left my cell and the time I returned. She spent one hour and twenty minutes with me. Mom you know Pence is president. Why are you not agreeing with me? She also told me to take a plea with the DA."

I really should have fired her. What possessed me to give her six chances is beyond me. Usually, after three strikes you are out with me.

Brian did start taking his medication but it certainly was not because Dr. Jacobs had control over him. He had actually agreed with Dr. Roman a few days before, but she had the need to take credit for everything. What a sad and very insecure person.

Dr. Roman and I spoke after Dr. Jacobs had visited Brian. He told me what Brian told him that Dr. Jacobs had said to him. I told him what she told us, and he said, "I was not sure if Brian was correct about the conversation. Did she say why she agreed with his delusions?" I told him, and he only sucked in his breath. I told Dr. Roman my opinion on the woman and left it at that.

Brian started coming around. Although he admitted he was depressed, he did not seem delusional OR he was hiding it very well. I visited him, and we had some great talks. I so wanted him well and out of there. We were fast approaching his December 18 court date. He was getting excited and asked if his dad and I would bail him out once he was declared competent. I started looking at facilities to put him in and get him well. No facility would take him if he was delusional and paranoid.

After speaking with Dr. Dunn and Jim, we could bail Brian out if he agreed to come home and get help. He had to agree to no pot smoking or steroids and that he would go to see Dr. Dunn twice a week. I proposed this to Brian, and he agreed. He just wanted out. Jim was still concerned. I did not blame him; I was too.

By this time, we had brought Brian's car home; most of his clothes were at our house. I had washed everything and hung up his clothes. Brian was still calling Simone, and she, bless her heart, was talking to him. He sent her letters. I did not pry into what was going on with them. It was not my business, although I did share with Brian how wonderful of a person she is. He did agree and said he loved her and always would.

December 18th was on a Monday. Jim and I stayed the night in San Diego at the Marriott close to the courthouse. We were both looking forward to seeing him and hopefully taking him home. The public defender was to meet us outside the courtroom.

We got there early and had some coffee and wondered how Brian was doing. You never knew what time the case would be called, so you had to wait. Once court was in session, we sat at the back of the room and saw Brian sit with the other inmates and wait his turn. He did not look happy, and I could not read his lips. A lady tapped me on the shoulder and asked if we were the Dubraskys. I said, "Yes." We followed her outside the courtroom into the hall, and she introduced herself as the supervisor of the public defender assigned to Brian's case. She then told us that Brian has been determined to be incompetent to stand trial by the court appointed psychologist. We were both shocked, as we were not expecting this, especially after the one we hired said that Brian may be delusional, but he knew what happens in court. We asked the supervisor if Brian knew, and she said that he did.

What happens now? Our son would now be ordered by the judge to take medication and to go to a treatment facility like Patterson in San Bernardino. I was so heartbroken. My baby was ordered by the court to go to a mental hospital. How can this be? How had he arrived at this place in his life? We did not have the option to post bail and get him out of there; he was in the hands of the court, which was making the decisions about his life.

So now, my son had spent Thanksgiving in jail and would also be spending Christmas and the New Year. I was angry, sad, upset, pissed, and furious. It was too much to bear; he did not deserve this. How much more were we and our beloved son expected to take? How could this be happening?

Jim and I left the courthouse, both dumbfounded as to what just took place. I know Brian was sick, but I wanted him home so we could take care of him.

We checked out of the hotel and drove back home. I drove, as it helped clear my head. Jim and I talked about what we could do, which seemed to be nothing at this point.

We arrived home, and as soon as I got inside the house, Brian called. He was screaming and yelling. I let him vent and got Jim on the phone too.

I was crying and so very sad for him. After a bit, he calmed down. Even he said, "How can the court be in charge of my life?" I had to agree with him but said, "Honey, take the medication. Talk to Dr. Roman and see what he thinks. Do you know how this is killing me, seeing you there? I never thought in a thousand years my Brian would be in jail at the mercy of the courts to determine your life."

Because Brian was so delusional, he was not thinking about how this was affecting us. We had sent him money, food, and books. I was driving down to visit him as often as I could. Instead of things getting better, they just seemed to be getting worse. I was on a roller-coaster that was not slowing down. It was going faster and faster and taking my breath way. I thought of Simone and how this was affecting her. Poor Simone, her life was turned upside down. The man she loved with all her being was in jail suffering from delusions and paranoia. On top of that, she moved and had to give Lola up, the dog she and Brian had adopted in July from a terrible situation. Her mother shared with me that the poor dog was put down when Joe took her back to the pound. The dog had bitten the woman at intake, who told Joe that she would have to be put down. Joe and Gina were so upset that they could not tell Simone, nor could I tell Brian. Every once in a while, he mentioned Lola. He told me as soon as he got out of there he was going to get her back. I did not have the heart to tell him that she was gone. My heart was so full, and even writing this, I am crying thinking of what we all had to endure.

    I scheduled a visit to see Brian when the schedule came up on the jail website. Because he was declared incompetent, his visiting hours had changed. We were close to Christmas, and I did not have the heart to do anything. I had no energy to even put up a tree. Why bother? I sent Michael and Quinnia a card with a check. I sent Brian a card but could put nothing in it for him. All I could do was wish him a Merry Christmas in jail (they don't have cards for that).

    I did not get to see him before Christmas, and the card I sent came back to me. I had not put the address on the card of the San Diego Central Jail. I was so out of it, I forgot to add it. So, my baby did not even get his card until after Christmas. During this time, he did not get to call because the jail was short staffed due to the holiday. Right after Christmas, I did get an appointment to see him, so off I went to San Diego.

I received a call from Dr. Roman on December 27, and he expressed his surprise at Brian being declared incompetent. He had relayed to me that even though Brian was delusional, he knew what goes on in court. He was aware of his charges and why he was there. He did tell me that Brian was on the list for JBCT (Jail Based Competency Treatment). He was also taking 5 mg of Zyprexa twice daily. In his opinion, Brian was getting better.

Brian was calm during our visit. I could see the medication was kicking in. We talked, and then he said to me, "Mom, I really want an attorney that can help me get out of here. The public defender does not care. They have so many cases. I am just a number to them. I promise to pay you and Dad back, but I need to get out of here. You know Patterson just lines you up and gives you medication twice a day. I am not a mental case like that. I am getting better." I said to my firstborn, "You know, your Dad and I will do whatever we can to help you. I have to make some calls and see what can be done. However, I don't think we can overturn anything the judge does. Talk to Dr. Roman and see what he says, OK?" He agreed. I thought and said, "Have you spoken with Dr. Roman? He likes you, and I know you trust him. He told me you are on the list for JBCT; hopefully, you won't have to go to Patterson." He said he was hoping so.

I drove home thinking about talking to Jim and researching criminal attorneys. All this was going on at the end of 2017. I was praying 2018 would be a much better year, and we could look back on the last quarter of 2017 as just a bad nightmare.

I Googled several attorneys in downtown San Diego. I received call backs and lost my voice explaining Brian's situation. Jim was not happy with the cost—a criminal attorney was not cheap. We now had to go into our retirement. At this point, I really did not care. All I wanted was for my son to be out of there and home. I so badly wanted him free and in charge of his life and whole again. Was that too much to ask? I prayed to God to give me my son back.

Brian was calling and told me it would be hard over the weekend with the New Year as the jail would be short staffed once again. Because of this, he hardly got to leave his cell to make a call. He had plenty of books to read and was still keeping in shape. He looked good every time I saw him; he still had his tan from all his hikes and surfing.

Jim and I hired an attorney just before the end of the year. He seemed good and honest. He did say something that resonated with me and was the reason I hired him: "You don't want your son to spend another holiday in jail, do you?" Of course I didn't. What mother or father would want that for their child?

Chapter Nine
January–March 2018

Happy New Year! I prayed this would be a wonderful year for us all! We could look back and say the previous year was just a bad dream.

Brian called a few days after the New Year. I told him we hired a criminal attorney, gave him the attorney's name, and told him to expect a visit from him soon. Brian was elated and thanked me and his dad. Again, he promised to pay us back and said he loved us very much. I told him I would come see him after I checked his schedule. He was worried about being sent to Patterson, and so was I. I could not imagine my Brian in a mental hospital.

Attorney Paulson (name has been changed) who we hired did indeed visit Brian. He spent time with him and got Brian's version of all that occurred. He never promised anything to Brian but said he would do all he could. He had Brian sign releases so he could talk to Brian's doctors, his parents (even though we were paying), and he even wanted to talk to Simone.

During this time, I spoke to Dr. Roman about getting Brian sent to the JBCT. Dr. Roman felt Brian was competent—even though he was somewhat delusional, he knew what was going on. He understood the process of the court

Brian's baptism. Proud mom and dad—notice how alert he is! May 1984

Three months old—always a smile.

One of my favorites, May 1984

Daddy and Brian, July 1984

Always a smile, July 1984

Brian at four months old with my brother, Michael

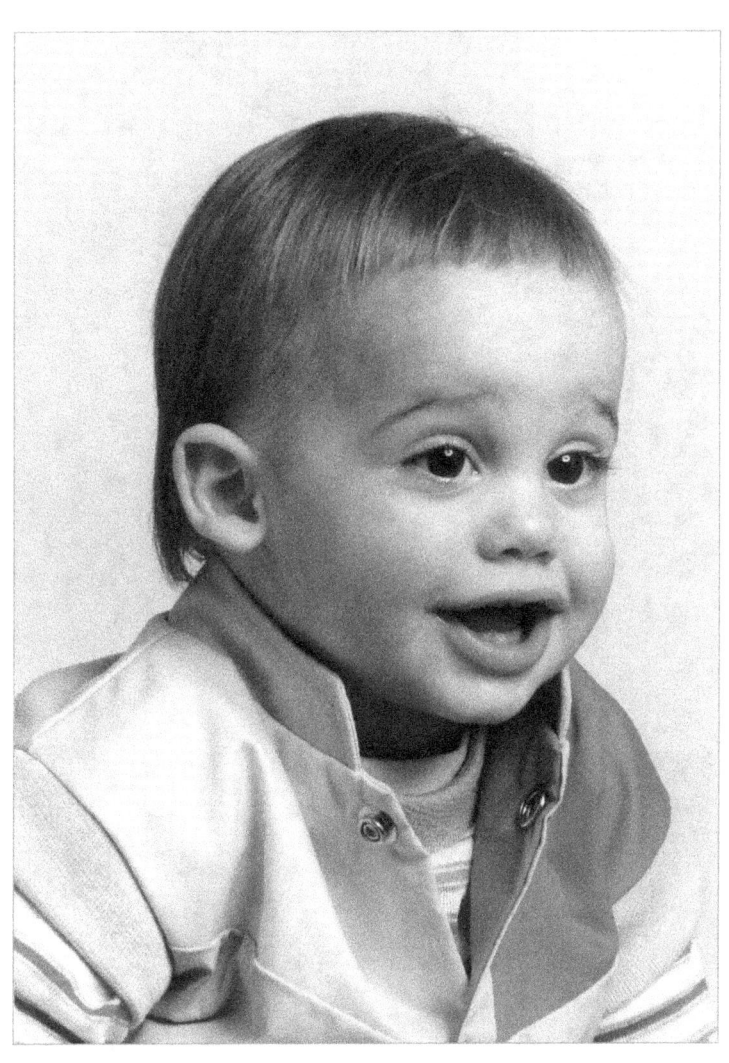
Brian at eleven months old

Before Michael was born. Brian coming to see mommy. February 1985

Brian and brother Michael

Mommy and her little men, Brian and Michael, 1986

Brian at age two. See the wing on the left of him?

At the beach with brother Michael and cousin Jesse, 1989

Brian and cousin Jesse, summer 1991

Acting photo

Brian and Michael, Christmas 1992

Fooling around during Christmas, 1995

Alaska, 1999

Family Vacation, last night on Maui, Hawaii, October 2002

Graduation Night. 2002

How he loved to eat!! May 2004

Brian and Tommy, Portugal, 2007

Brian and Tommy, Prague, 2007

*Brian and me, his birthday in San Diego,
CA, March 18, 2014*

Brian with Casper, 2015

Brian and Simone, La Jolla, CA, July 2017

Brian and Simone before he got sick, September 2017

and was doing well on the medication (Zyprexa). Brian had expressed to me that he read in medical books in the jail library that Zyprexa can cause suicidal thoughts. It hurt to hear him say that, so all I could say was, "Honey, you are on a very small dose. Talk to Dr. Roman if you are concerned, OK?" All he said was "Yeah."

It seemed we were making progress that first few weeks. Brian had his psychiatrist, Dr. Roman, on his side and Paulson was moving forward with obtaining all the information on his case. I seemed able to breathe again and looked forward to Brian being home soon.

Paulson called and asked for the report from the independent psychologist that we hired for Brian, Dr. Jacobs. I did not have a report; she never gave us one. She felt she would write a "juicy one" if and when the time came. I told him this, and he asked me to get it for him. He felt it was crucial to the case to have an independent psychologist that declared him competent back in December, especially one that was hired independently from the court-appointed psychologist.

I left her a message, and she responded that she was out of state on a case and could not give me a report at that time. I told her we had hired a criminal attorney for Brian, and he just wanted something from her saying that in her opinion Brian was competent to stand trial. Rather than say she would do this, she started giving me a hard time. She was a difficult person to deal with, and finally I had to threaten her with reporting her to the Board of Psychology. She finally relented and asked for Paulson's contact information and said she would deal with him. I said, "Fine, do that, but just remember you were paid for services rendered and a report was part of that, which we never received." Her behavior was shocking, and even Dr. Dunn was aghast at her attitude.

Needless to say, Paulson was also shocked at her attitude in giving a report. She started texting him and badmouthing me, and instead of a report, she wrote a long email slamming me but did say in her opinion Brian was competent. This was in no way a formal report, just an email that was not professional at all. Paulson being a professional, and an attorney at that, did not say much about it but did agree she had issues with giving a professional report. In the meantime, she was texting him late at night asking what was going on with Brian. He never responded. It was none of her business.

The third week of January, Brian was sent to the Jail Based Competency Treatment. Yes! Dr. Roman and the medical doctor did everything they could to get Brian there. It was still in the jail, but he was moved to another medical floor and still considered a medical patient. He was in classes all day as to what went on in court, who was who. Brian already knew all this and turned out to be a model student. Dr. Roman called me several times to report that Brian was doing very well. I continued to visit him, and he seemed more at peace. He did say that he was depressed and that the medication made him very sleepy. He slept a lot but did enjoy the classes, even though he already knew what he was learning.

I continued to send him food and money for calls. He did call Michael a few times, but with Michael's work schedule it was hard to get in touch with him. Michael was so sad about his brother being in jail. He would call me and ask me for an update. I did not want to bother Michael too much since he had his wife and a new puppy. He got her an emotional support animal, and it was helping. The addition to their family was wonderful. I loved the pictures they sent. Lady Beatrix was beautiful, and I could not wait to meet her! My doggie granddaughter!

Paulson was doing a fine job. Brian liked him and felt good about him, as did Jim and I. All we had to do was wait for Brian to finish his classes, and then the jail would send that report to court and a new court date would be scheduled.

February, a new month was upon us. I went to see Brian one Sunday morning and left before the sun was up. It occurred to me my son had not been outside since his CT scan months ago. I took a picture of the sun rising. I was not supposed to take my phone into the jail with me, but I thought, What the heck? I showed Brian the pictures I took, and he looked at them through the glass and said he could not wait to smell the air and see the sun rising and setting again. I told him, "Soon my son, you will be free and all this will be just a bad memory. I am proud of how you handled it all; you are a champ." He seemed down but was talkative. He told me the deputy had to wake him for my visit. I said I was sorry, but I liked coming with no traffic and getting home by mid-afternoon. That day, instead of only thirty minutes, we got to talk for a full hour. The deputy was not rushing us at all. Finally, the call ended, and I blew Brian a kiss, and he blew me one.

I was feeling excited on the way home and thanked God for all his answers. My son would be coming home soon. Jim and I would take him to all his favorite restaurants: Mr. Sushi, Wokcano, Pei Wei, Larsen's, and Spumoni.

I called Simone and Gina and told them Brian was

coming around. He had finished his classes, and a new court date would be scheduled soon.

I was looking up Brian's court date every day, and he was calling me when he could. Finally, he had a court date of February 14th. I was so happy and over the moon. I could not wait to hear from Brian and left a message for Paulson.

When Brian called and he told me the court date, I asked him how he was, and he said, "Excited to get out of here." I asked him if he needed anything from the commissary until he got out, and he said no and thanked me. He really seemed OK but something was off. I could not put my finger on it, and his voice inflection was not as excited as I thought he would be.

I called and texted all his buddies and told them he would be home on February 15, and we would have a party as soon as he was settled. Charles texted back to let him know when he was out and that Casper missed him. All his friends knew what was going on; Charles kept them all apprised of Brian's situation. I promised Charles a phone call before we left San Diego so he could talk to Brian.

Jim and I went out and bought underwear, shaving items, and socks for Brian. I made sure his room was ready for him. I had cleared out my belongings; the guest room was now Brian's. I was a happy camper my son was coming home! Life was good, praise the Lord!

I booked the Marriott in downtown San Diego for Tuesday, February 13th through the 15th. I would book a room for Brian once we knew more at court.

Jim and I had a lovely dinner that night, and what I did not eat I saved for Brian. He always loved salmon, and I can never eat a full meal. I knew he would enjoy it. The rooms had a refrigerator and microwave.

That morning, we went to a bail bonds place close to the courthouse and told them we would be posting bail. At this point we were hoping Paulson could get the bail reduced from $50,000 to a lot less, especially since he had served four-and-a-half months.

We walked to the courthouse, both of us quiet and praying all would go well for Brian and that we could get him released.

Paulson met us outside the courtroom. He said the report had come in from the jail, and Brian was declared competent. He said he would ask for a reduction in bail, and we would most likely be taking him home that day once he was released and the bond posted. I cried with joy! I know Jim was a little apprehensive about Brian but I was not. I just wanted him home to take care of him.

We saw Brian in court, and he gave me the "thumbs-up." He smiled and sat next to Paulson and did not say anything. Paulson asked for a reduction in bail, but the DA said "no," that considering Brian's charges, he would not reduce bail! Paulson replied, "He has already spent over four months in jail; all I am asking is for a reduction." The DA still responded with a "NO." Okay, so what—we would still get our son out at any cost. What's money, anyway?

Brian was headed back to the holding room and gave me another "thumbs-up" with a smile. I did the same. I knew he would call me as soon as he got back, when he could.

We thanked Paulson and left to go to the bail bondsman to arrange the bail. The bondsman told us once bail was posted, it would still be quite some time before he was released. "How long?" I asked. He said, "It could be around 10:00 p.m. this evening or even later. I promise to call you as soon as I post the bond and know more." We thanked him and left.

I called Simone and told her the news. She was happy, and I said, "Honey, are you working? Would you like to spend the night here once we get Brian? I know he would love to see you. What do you think?" She said she would let me know; she did want to see Brian.

We had free time until we got the calls. I was exhausted. I finally felt like a noose had been released from my neck. I could only imagine what my beautiful son felt. Still, he was inside waiting. At 3:30 p.m. he called me, and we spoke. He said he could not wait to get out of there, and I said it could take some time. I told him what the bondsman told us. I assured him the bond was in place and relayed what Paulson told us about coming back for another court date in March and hopefully getting credit for time served. There would be so much to think about after he was out, but right now I was not contemplating any of that.

We were playing the waiting game, yet again! We walked around with my phone, and I tried to rest but could not. Simone called and said she would love to be there for Brian. I booked a room for her and Brian just down the hall from us. I also told her it would be late before he was released.

True to his word, the bondsman called and told us it was going to be much longer. The judges had released over eighty inmates that day, due to it being Valentine's Day. He said it most likely will be after midnight. "Really, they release these poor inmates in the middle of the night?" He said, "Yes, they do; that is how our jail system works." I was appalled. He said to wait for the jail to call you to go pick up your son.

I made sure my cell was charged and on a high ring volume. I met Simone in the lobby and gave her the room key. She was tired but excited as well to see Brian outside of the glass in the jail. She and I each had a glass of wine before we went back to our rooms. I hugged her and thanked her for being there. I so loved this beautiful woman; she had been through so much since September. She never complained, but I knew she was hoping Brian was back to himself. She knew she could come see him anytime while he was with us.

I had packed a bag of clothes for Brian. I had his wallet and driver's license and put $100 in there for him. Jim brought a warm sweat jacket for Brian, as it gets cold in the night at that time of year.

I tried to fall asleep to no avail. I lay there and kept looking at the clock. I wondered what Brian was going through. He had told me so much in these past months of the treatment in jail. I wondered if it was true or if it was his delusions and paranoia talking. Some of those things I could not get out of my mind:

> No hot water in the showers
>
> No toilet paper for five days and how he had to wipe himself
>
> Inmate phones broken for months
>
> A deputy was verbally abusing the inmates
>
> TV was off in December due to no batteries in the remote

These are the ones that stuck out in my mind. It was just

awful. Still looking at the clock: 1:00 a.m., 1:15 a.m., 2:00 a.m., 2:20 a.m., 2:24 a.m. What the hell?

I could not sleep while Jim was lying next to me slightly snoring. I lay there; I could not wait to hug my baby again. 3:00 a.m., 3:29 a.m., and finally at 3:30 a.m., the call: "I have a Brian Dubrasky that would like a ride." I was overjoyed! I replied, "We will be right there." I called for the car and woke Jim. I texted Simone and said he would be there soon.

We got in our car, and I drove the five blocks to pick up Brian. There he was standing outside, trying to keep warm with just a pair of shorts, a white tee-shirt, and a pair of flip-flops. He jumped in the back seat, and Jim gave him the sweatshirt. He said, "It is freezing out there." We agreed, and he said, "It was a zoo there with all the releases. I was up since 11:00 in a holding room just waiting." I told him what the bondsman told us: eighty releases that day. Brian was so happy to be out, and I asked him how he felt. He said, "Free at last." I noticed that Brian had no paperwork or any of the books or drawings. I did ask him, and he said the jail gave him nothing! I thought that was strange, but my son was out, so no bother. We would take care of that later, especially his prescription for Zyprexa.

We got back to the hotel, and I ran around to Brian and gave him a huge hug. I was so happy to have him back. I told him so. We walked inside, and the lobby was quiet and warm. Brian stopped midway and said, "I have a mental disorder." I will never forget that; it still haunts me. All I said was "Sweetheart, you will get better. That is why you are coming home. Simone is in the room waiting for you." He said, "She's here?" "Yes, sweetheart, she is here waiting for you." He seemed quite pleased. He would not be alone in the room.

He came to our room, and I gave him his bag of clothes and shoes. I also gave him his wallet and said, "Honey, your license expires this year. Did you know that?" He said, "Really?" I hugged him and walked him to his room where Simone was waiting. I remember hugging him again before he went into the room. "I love you, sweetheart. Get some rest; we will meet for breakfast. We have to go to the bondsman on the way out as you have to sign some papers." "Oh sweetheart, please eat the salmon I left in the fridge. I know you love salmon, and you can microwave it." Inside he went to be with his darling, Simone. I was glad he was not alone.

I awoke at 8:00 a.m. I had already received a text from Simone saying they were up and walking around. She asked what time we should meet for breakfast. "9:00 okay with you and Brian?" She texted back, "Sure, meet you in the hotel restaurant."

Jim is not an early riser, but he got up and we quickly showered. I needed coffee and to see my son. We had a full day ahead of us, and I wanted to get started. I made a note to call Charles after Brian signed the paperwork, and we were on our way home.

Jim and I sat down and ordered coffee and omelets. Simone said they were on their way.

I looked up and saw Brian and Simone. First thought in my mind: he was in the same clothes he walked out of jail with. He had on the flip-flops and apparently had not taken a shower. I wondered why? I would think after four months he would stand in a hot shower for a long time. No bother, there has to be an explanation.

Brian and Simone came to sit down. Simone sat next to me, and Brian kept standing and said, "I want a beer." Jim and I looked at him and said, "Honey, you can't drink on that medication you are taking." He looked at us and said, "I need to use the bathroom." He left, and Simone and I started talking. She ordered steak and eggs for them both. I asked her what they had been doing, and she said they had been walking outside the hotel and talking.

It was after 9:15 a.m., and they had gotten to the restaurant at 9:00 a.m.. Our food was ordered and would be coming soon. I said to Jim, "Brian's been gone a while. Can you go check on him?" Simone said he was OK and not to worry. I was worried; something was wrong. Jim came back and said Brian was not in the bathroom. Simone said she would go check the room. Our food came, and I had one bite. I knew something was up. Where in the world was Brian? Simone came back down and said he was not in the room. Jim had a few bites of his omelet, got up and left to check outside for Brian, came back, and no Brian.

Jim and Simone were at the table with me when our waitress said, "A guy just jumped from the building across the street." My heart went in my throat. I knew. Simone said, "No, it's not Brian." The waitress said, "This guy had on beige shorts and a sweat jacket." I jumped up, and as I was walking I felt such a jolt pass through my body. I knew—I knew it was my son!

Jim was already across the street talking to a policeman. I could see a body covered up with a yellow tarp. I was crying and praying that it not be my Brian, but I knew. I got there and saw his feet; that is all I could see was my son's feet. The officer asked us who we were, and then Simone was beside me. We gave him Brian's name and told him Brian should have his wallet on him. The officer looked at Simone and asked who she was. She told him his girlfriend. The officer asked for any tattoos or piercings. She told him.

I wanted to see my son, but Jim said, "No, honey, you don't want to see him that way."

We waited what seemed like hours, and then the officer came back and told Jim it was Brian. I fell down sobbing with Simone. Jim was holding me, and then a policewoman walked us to the police car. We all sat inside the back crying and sobbing. I kept saying over and over again…"My baby, my baby, why?" Hearing Jim and Simone cry was gut wrenching. A police woman gave us some waters, and then I heard her say, "Oh no, the press is here." She went away, and the three of us sat crying and hugging each other. We sat in that car for quite some time before the medical examiner came and introduced herself. I can still see her face but cannot remember her name. She was a very pleasant lady and seemed so young. She did ask where we were staying, and Jim told her. She asked us if we could all meet in our room after she looked at Brian. Jim said yes and gave her our room number.

Our world as we knew it was shattered beyond belief. Nothing was the same or ever would be again. I looked over and saw my son lying on the cold concrete with a yellow tarp covering his body except for his feet. Life as we knew it was forever changed in a fraction of a second.

I cannot remember if I called Gina or if Simone did. But she and Joe were there pretty fast. Simone kept saying she wanted to go home. Gina and Joe hugged me and Jim, crying. By this time, we were in the room, and Jim followed Simone, Gina, and Joe to the room she had shared with Brian. Jim said he would get his bag and be right back.

Some lovely ladies came by the room—grief counselors—and sat with me. I just remember having to use the bathroom so badly, and I sat on the toilet for ages. I was crying so hard, and all of a sudden, a calmness overcame me and a voice inside my head said, "You can do this." I spoke to the lovely ladies, and then the medical examiner came. Jim had come back from Brian's room. The medical examiner gave Jim a brown paper bag with Brian's wallet and cell phone. They gave us all the information on where they were taking Brian and what we had to do. I just wanted to go home, like Simone. I wanted to get the hell out of San Diego and go home!

After we were alone, I told Jim I wanted to get out of there. We both packed, and when we checked out, the receptionist gave us her condolences. She said our meal had been paid for. Oh my God, I forgot about the waitress. I saw her from a distance and ran over to her and gave her a tip and thanked her. She hugged me and said how very sorry she was.

We got to our car, and then I remembered we had to see the bondsman. Jim was driving, and on the way there, Charles called. I picked up the phone, and he said, "Can I talk to Brian?" I told him, and he said "Please tell me you are joking." He was crying and I was crying, and I told him we had to go to the bondsman. We promised to call each other later.

The bondsman was so sweet and caring. He said this had never happened to him before. He told us to take care and to please email him a copy of Brian's death certificate. When he mentioned the death certificate, I started crying again, and Jim helped me to the car. Nothing was the same; everything felt different and distant now. No color anywhere, it was so bleak, though it was a beautiful morning in downtown San Diego. I knew then that I would never look at anything the same way ever again. My life had changed in an instant. My son was gone—not here on this earth anymore.

It was only 12:00 p.m., and I felt like I had been up for a week. I was mentally and physically exhausted. We needed gas, and I remembered telling Jim where to go to get it before we hit the freeway.

While Jim was pumping the gas, my mind was on Michael. How do we tell our youngest that his brother is gone? My heart was aching and bleeding for both my sons, for Simone, for Jim, for me. It was the hardest thing I've ever been through. Losing a brother, two sisters, my mom, my nephew, and my dad was all hard enough but my own son? I sat in the car and thought of memories of Brian when he was little and smiled at all his cute sayings. I thought of him and his brother playing and laughing. My head was swimming, and it would not stop. I was now a grieving mother. My heart had been ripped out from my body; my beloved son was no longer in this world with us. Who was the first person he saw upon entering the other side? Was my mother there to greet him? Jim's mom, Mimi? Who was there to help my son cross over? So many thoughts raced through my mind while Jim was pumping gas.

Finally, Jim got back into the car. I said to Jim, "How are we going to tell our Michael?" He said, "Let's wait until we get home." "OK," I said.

As Jim was driving, I was watching the road and really looked at all the details of the road. I saw all the cars passing us by and thought, "Don't they know I've lost a son this morning? They are all going about their business and have no idea how I am grieving."

I then thought of calling Dr. Dunn and telling him he would not be treating Brian but that I needed to see him. I called his office, and he called me back. He was so sad and kept saying how sorry he was. I made an appointment, and then the calls started coming from Brian's friends. Ryan called and was so upset and sad—he was crying. Then it occurred to me to tell him not to post anything on Facebook, as we had not spoken to Michael yet. I did not want our youngest to see it on Facebook before we told him. Ryan promised he would reach out to everybody and ask them to not post yet.

I called my sister Diane and told her and asked her to let Gail and the rest of the family know. She cried with me and offered her support.

I needed to use the restroom, and I remembered we stopped at McDonald's in Mission Viejo. I was drinking water because my mouth was dry from all the crying. Jim got something to eat; he had not finished his omelet, and being a big man, he needs to eat. I could not think of food. All I could think of was that my Brian would never eat another meal. He loved food and always ate with such gusto. We would not be taking him to all his favorite restaurants.

We were about thirty minutes from home when our Michael called, and we were going through La Tuna Canyon where cell service is generally cut off. I answered and told Michael we would be losing phone service, so we would call as soon as we got home.

I had to go to the bathroom again and asked Jim to stop at a McDonald's. We stopped in San Fernando. Jim got a little something to eat and said to me, "Darling, you need to eat." I said, "I can't. Water is fine." I could not tell him that all I could think about is that our son would never eat again; it pained me. When I closed my eyes, all I could see was his feet and his body covered in a yellow tarp on the sidewalk.

After we got home and brought our stuff in, we called Michael. That was the hardest call for both of us. Jim got on the speaker of my phone and said, "Michael, what we have to tell you is not easy. Are you sitting down?" Michael replied, "Yes, what happened?" "We did bail your brother out yesterday, picked him up at 3:30 this morning and only had a little time with him. He took his life by jumping off a building across the street from the hotel." Jim proceeded to give him details. I heard Michael over the phone asking questions. I knew he would be sad and in shock. It would take a while to sink in; I was still in disbelief.

After our call to Michael, I called some of my close friends and told them the sad news. What I could not say was that Brian died by suicide and that he had been in jail. I only said he was in the hospital in San Diego after a mental breakdown. I don't know why I could not bring myself to tell my friends, especially some very close friends. It pained me to say it and even pained me more that my darling son took his own life.

I walked into Brian's room and sat on the bed and cried and cried. I was so looking forward to his being home. I was going to cook his favorite meals, take him out, and help him get well. What would I do now? My beloved firstborn was gone, gone way too soon.

I got up and unpacked, and then I remembered the brown paper bag with his wallet and cell phone. I opened it as the tears were falling from my face. There was his wallet and driver's license, cracked cell phone. It was too much to bear. I looked into the wallet, and the money I put in there was still there. I pulled it out and counted it. There was $120, but I had only given him $100. How could that be? I went downstairs and told Jim. He said the jail most likely gave him a $20.

That made sense. I put Brian's wallet and cell phone in one of his drawers.

Evening was approaching, and the sun was going down. I sat for hours in his room on the bed crying. Jim came up and said he felt as if our future had been torn away. I knew exactly what he meant. It was indeed. Nothing would ever be the same again.

I remember finally succumbing to sleep that night. It was a dreamless sleep, an abyss. I woke up and immediately thought of Brian. I looked at the clock and it was 7:30 a.m., less than twenty-four hours since my son passed.

For some reason, after I awoke, I looked into Brian's room, where my son was supposed to be. I noticed the bed looked as if someone had lain down on the comforter, the pillows were askew as well. Then I remembered that I had sat on the bed crying yesterday. But I did not sit by the pillows. Strange.

I made my coffee and sat there crying. I had to let it out and kept asking, "Why?" I cried so hard I could not breathe and had to take a deep breath. I ached all over, and my heart actually hurt. It was the worst pain I have ever felt. Was I having a heart attack? No, it's called *grief*.

I had put the paperwork the medical examiner gave us on my desk. I was not ready to go through it but knew I had to. Brian had expressed after his cousin, Jesse, passed way that he wanted to be cremated if he passed before his dad and me. I looked at the list of mortuaries and remember thinking to myself, I've just lost a son and now I have to take care of his remains and still go on with my life.

Jim got up, and after he ate and had his coffee, we discussed all we needed to do. We made a list of what was most important to least important. We had to decide on a mortuary/crematory first. I only called one place. I was not going to worry about costs. The lady who answered was very consoling, and I knew I picked the right place. She sent me an email with what she needed for Brian's death certificate.

Filling out your son's death certificate does not seem right. This is not the way it is supposed to happen. Brian and Michael were the executors of our living trust; they were supposed to take care of burying us and getting rid of our belongings. Jim and I took care of our parents. Then I remembered that my mother had lost two children before she passed. Gail had lost Jesse, and now I had lost Brian. They did it, and I could do it. Mom always said, "God gives you what you can handle." I can do this. Take one day at a time.

I managed to get the paperwork done and sent it along with the payment. Next was writing Brian's obituary. I had written my mother's back in 2004 and my brother's in 1984. I would start it and have Jim add what he wanted to say and needed to say as a father who had just lost a son.

Friday afternoon, one day after Brian passed away, we had an appointment with Dr. Dunn. We both needed to talk to him and get some advice. As usual, he gave us great advice. There was nothing we could have done or said to change Brian's mind. We did everything we could do, and we had to remember that. Grief is so personal and we needed to make sure we took time to grieve. Jim and I needed to support each other and talk about our feelings. What I have always loved about Dr. Dunn is that he practices cognitive therapy: thoughts, feelings, and beliefs. I can still see Jim and me sitting on the sofa in his office, holding each other and crying. We went through a whole box of Kleenex, as I recall.

I had to post something on Facebook about Brian. I sat to write something from my heart, posted it, and cried again. How sad, I thought, that my wonderful son had to spend the last four-and-a-half months being incarcerated and not in his right mind. I was so distraught. I kept thinking, I wish my mom were here. She was so strong and had been through so much in her life. She always had the best advice. Move on, Janet, I said to myself. You can do this.

My cousin in Australia texted me that my Uncle Brian would be calling; he had something to tell me. I had a feeling he was ill, but Sharmain wanted him to tell me.

On the Saturday after Brian passed, I received a package from Amazon with three books on grief. Our friend Stacey had sent them; how sweet and kind of her. I sent her a text thanking her. Flowers started arriving as well as a fruit basket. Patti and Mark, Tommy's mom and stepdad, came by with food for us. I still was not eating much at all. Mark told us we were the first to drop food off after Tommy; they never forgot.

Brian's friends were texting me and asking if they could do anything. I always said he had the best of friends in his life.

My uncle called on Saturday and told me he had been diagnosed with lung cancer. He was eighty-seven and told me he had done all he wanted to do, and the good Lord had given him this long. I cried and told him how much I loved him. He told me he would never forget that Jim and I had come to visit him. I told him, "It's not goodbye, but see you later." He laughed.

Jim and I spoke about doing a celebration of Brian's life, we had to for his friends and us. We all needed this. Brian's thirty-fourth birthday was to be on March 18th, so

I said what about then with a cake and balloons. We called Michael and asked him what he thought and if he could get away from work. We all decided it would be a nice time to celebrate Brian's life. Now, where would we have it? I knew Stacey would have ideas, so I called her and she mentioned several venues. I wanted something nice and elegant for Brian.

I had so many balls in the air, but keeping busy helped me move. If I did not move I would just put the blanket over my head and stay in bed. I had to keep going for Jim and Michael. Yes, I wanted to be with my Brian in heaven, but I had to finish what I have to do in this life, my journey on earth.

I started reading a book that Stacey had sent us, *Dying to Be Free* by Beverly Cobain and Jean Larch. I could not put it down. It was so healing and exactly what Dr. Dunn had told us: "It's not our fault." I found the "Connections" chapter to be fascinating and kept talking to Brian to send me a sign that he was all right and had arrived in a beautiful place. I knew he would when he could.

Through all this, I was talking to and texting with Simone and her mom, Gina. I was very concerned for Simone and how she was grieving. The loss was hard for me, but she was his girlfriend and lover. She knew Brian in a totally different way than we did. My heart went out to her and all she went through those four-and-a-half months while he was incarcerated.

Danny and Carly asked us to come by the Friday a week and a day after our son passed away. They live in Lake Elizabeth, just a thirty-minute drive. We offered to take pizza and wine.

We arrived, and Danny presented us with a portrait of Brian that he drew after he heard what happened. He told us, "I felt Brian while I was drawing, and I hope you like it." Did we like it? My heart swelled with gratitude and joy. I felt my son and knew he was there with us.

Ryan, Krystle, Eddie, and Krysta dropped by to offer condolences. They wanted to hear what happened. I told the story while Jim held my hand and filled in when I got too choked up. I was so happy my son had these wonderful friends who cared about him so much. I learned a lot about him that night. Each of them had a funny story to tell and then a more serious one about our beloved. What a guy; I always knew he was special. He was thoughtful and compassionate. Krysta told us that one time her mother and stepfather were fighting, and she had to get away. She told us, "Brian always said if I needed a place to stay to let him know. It was horrible. I texted Brian, and he said come on over, you only live a few blocks from me. So I did, and Brian slept on the floor and gave me his bed. Not many men would do that. He had a heart of gold." My heart ached hearing her story. It made me sad that she had endured hearing her mom and stepdad argue. Jim and I thanked them all and told them when Brian's celebration would be but that we did not know where yet.

There is one thing about that night I will never forget. Danny and Carly have a beautiful dog, Stevie. Stevie lay under my chair at the table whilst I told them about Brian. When I moved to sit on the sofa, Stevie followed me and lay her head on my leg. She was comforting me and knew that I was a grieving mother. How profound that a dog knows.

Saturday morning after our evening with Danny and Carly, exactly one week and two days after Brian passed,

I woke up and looked down. There by my side of the bed was a shiny penny. I cried, and then I started laughing. I knew it was from my son, letting me know he had arrived in a good place. I picked it up and showed Jim and said, "Is there one by you?" There was not; this was for both of us. I was now crying tears of joy.

I hung the picture that Danny drew of Brian right across from our family portrait. As I was looking at the portrait, I noticed that the background of rays of light was in a painting that Jim and I had bought in Hawaii. Did Danny know that? He must have seen the painting, or did he just envision Brian with those rays of light behind him?

Simone texted me that Brian's workplace wanted to do a celebration at the bar in San Diego at the end of February. An invite was sent via Facebook, and when I read what they wrote, I broke down. I really did not want to drive back to San Diego, but we needed to attend. Brian had made a new life for himself in San Diego and with Simone. As hard as it would be for us, we would be there. While there, we could pick up his death certificate, which neither of us relished doing.

Our son certainly had some fabulous friends, and his coworkers were so complimentary about their friend. Brian's boss, Ritchie, took care of everything, and to this day I am so honored that he did that. It was an absolutely beautiful celebration. What a testament to our beloved son and his generous and kind soul. At sunset, we all went to the beach and set off balloons in our son's honor. The Lord graced us with a magnificent sunset. Jim and I sat on the concrete wall for a long time just gazing at the sunset. My son was there; I just know he was.

The next morning, we stopped by the crematory and picked up Brian's death certificate. Jim and I sat in the car and opened the envelope and both cried and hugged each other. There are no words to express how we both felt: such a tremendous sense of loss and heartache. It was like the axis of our world was spinning opposite of the way it was supposed to.

The next few weeks flew by with getting our son's celebration planned.

Jim and I met with the event coordinator at the Valencia Country Club. It was exactly what I thought would be a nice venue. Patti had Tommy's celebration of life there. The room had a lovely view of the golf course, and there was a reception area to greet guests. Having eaten there, we knew the food was good, and the club said we could bring in a cake and balloons. We got the date set, put down the deposit, and left.

Social media is nice in some ways and not so nice in others. I was quite upset when I read that an acquaintance of Brian's actually posted about his suicide. It was not her place to post, and I let her know via Messenger to take it down. She had Brian and Simone's picture and said with a caption, "This is how depression looks." Wow! I let Ryan and Danny know and asked if they knew her; they told me they did. They would let her know that what she did was inappropriate.

Michael and Quinnia booked their flight to come in for ten days. I was happy they could spend some time and not rush back. I desperately needed my baby son around. They would be bringing their new puppy with them since she is an emotional support animal. We could not wait to meet her.

We needed an officiator for the celebration. I called Stacey (my go-to person), and she said she would ask around. Jim said he could do it, but I did not feel he should, especially since he was the grieving father.

I ordered the cake along with the balloons. My friend Cindi asked what she could do to help, and I mentioned the table arrangements—nothing fancy, but since the tables were for ten people, we needed something.

Jim and I continued seeing Dr. Dunn, and I was reading my books about grieving, which were so helpful. Reading what others wrote who had lost a child to suicide was so sad. The shock we all have to endure afterward is unconscionable. I had time to prepare with my brother and mother; knowing they were going to pass was still hard but a bit easier. You get to say what you want to say before they pass. I never got to do that with Brian. I am so glad I hugged him, but I did not get to spend time eating a meal with him. I always loved seeing him eat; he loved food and always ate with such passion. He truly enjoyed the experience of good food.

I needed to get the pictures for the montage. Charles had offered to help put it together for us. Jim and I were working on the program. We also had to work on what we would want the officiator to say during the celebration. Since Jim loved writing, he helped do a lot of that. I asked Quinnia if she could do an invite that we could send out via text, email, or Messenger. We only wanted Brian's good friends there, our friends, and what little family we had left. All in all, we were looking at eighty to one hundred attendees.

Three weeks after my beloved son passed, I finally decided to go for a walk. I had stopped walking after Brian passed and felt I needed to go for a walk. I walked down to the park and sat down on the bench by the roses. It was a beautiful early March—birds chirping, squirrels running around, and the air was so fresh. I cried and cried. I was so stuffed up and forgot Kleenex. I had to get back before Jim got worried. As I was slowly walking back, I saw a beautiful white feather at my feet. It was not there before, as I was retracing my footsteps home. Of course it was Brian, and I said, "Thank you, my angel, for letting me know you are still around in spirit." I felt him beside me on the walk home. How comforting is that?

I texted all of Brian's friends, asking if anybody wanted something of Brian's. Not that I wanted to get rid of Brian's possessions, but I knew his friends would want a reminder of their friend. We had his car, and since we did not need it, we reached out to Michael to see if he wanted it.

I sat in the garage going through pictures. I had so many albums of our sons, and it was so hard going through them—such great memories of their childhood. I was grateful that Brian had written his reflections of his life and his thoughts of his amazing childhood.

As I sat there in the garage, I picked up a box of Jim's mother's belongings and opened it. I went through the small photo album she had and noticed a picture of Brian I had never seen before. He was two, and Mimi had given him a cup with two candles on it that he was blowing out. It was so adorable and an outfit I remember very vividly. But what attracted my attention was on the very side of him was what appeared to be an angel wing! I kept looking at it, and it hit me. My son was with the angels in heaven and led me to this picture that I had never seen. I sat there for a long time and cried and thanked Brian for leading me to it. I took that picture and showed Jim; he was amazed as well.

I carefully placed it on the portrait that Danny gave us, as a constant reminder that my son had his angel wings even at two years old. I always knew he was a special soul, and this confirmed it to me.

Everything was slowly getting into place for March 18th. I felt that Brian was happy with all our decisions. I texted his friends Ryan, Brandon, Danny, Matt, and Charles and asked if they would speak at the celebration. All texted back; they were happy to do so and were honored. Michael would be the first to speak on behalf of his brother. Obviously, Simone and her parents would attend, and we offered that she could speak if she felt able.

We got the program printed up, and Jim sat down and wrote what the officiator would say. We had found a wonderful pastor through one of Stacey's friends. We met Pastor Phil and were so delighted that he could do it on the date we had set.

Cindi called and told me the flowers she had found via the internet were charging more than our budget. I thanked her and said I would find something. For some reason, the thought of indoor plants that the guests could take with them afterward came into my head. I went to Valencia Florist and found exactly what I had seen in my head. We could do three to four plants on each table in the center. Brian would like that better than flowers.

One evening, while Jim and I were sitting discussing the upcoming celebration for Brian, the TV came on by itself. We both looked at each other to see who had the remote; neither of us did. I believe it was a sign that our son was there in spirit. Jim was quite dumbfounded until I said, "It's Brian. I know it is."

Every night, I would ask Brian to come tell me what happened. I so desperately needed to know what happened to his mind. Was it the steroids? Pot? Hit on the head? What caused my baby to take his life? I always felt he had his act together; he was so smart and could do anything he set his mind to. He had so much to offer, so why? Sometimes I would wake up after being in an abyss, a void—no answers, just more questions. I started finding some more books that would help that were about life beyond death. I had to know more about the other side, our soul journey.

Ryan came by first to pick out a few of Brian's clothes. I was so happy that his friends all wanted something of my son's. I could smell Brian on his black leather jacket. Ryan took all the new underwear and some shirts and shoes, as he and Brian were the same size. Danny came next and was so delighted to get some of the shirts, T-shirts, and sweatshirts. Matt came by and got a pair of shoes that looked like they had never been worn. I figured I could donate what was left to a homeless shelter.

Michael did not want the car. He already had two, so what would he do with a third? Good point. I got his opinion as to what we should do with it. He mentioned that we could ask Brian's friends if anybody wanted it. We asked Ryan, and he said that he would be happy to take it, and how much? We could not take any money; we just wanted to give it to someone who would take care of it. Ryan was so grateful and thanked us profusely. We said we would clean it up for him first.

Ryan later called and told us that he really felt Danny should have it because he needed a car badly. He would have Danny come by and look at it and let us know. Well, we were so happy that Danny wanted it and needed it. After all he had done for us—the beautiful portrait of our son, having us over to tell them all what happened—it felt right. We knew Brian was happy, and we called it the BriMobile. We told Danny we would all have to go to Triple A to transfer the title, and it was a gift from Brian to him. But since the celebration was so close, we wanted to allow Michael to use it while he was here. All agreed.

Michael, Quinnia, and Lady Beatrix arrived four days before Brian's celebration. It was so nice having them, though the reason for their visit was devastating. I fell in love with my grandpuppy. She ran all over the place and was so comforting to have around. The love a dog gives is without asking for anything in return, except to love them and feed them. Lady knew I was grieving, just like Stevie did, and sat on my lap to lick me. She was comforting and loving.

I still was not eating much, just enough to keep me going. I wanted to cook Michael's favorite meals and especially his all-time favorite, chicken Dijon. I showed Quinnia how to make it and managed to get a few bites in. They wanted to go see some of Michael's friends, so they left Lady with us. She was a doll, and I enjoyed getting to know her. She quickly learned that she was very much welcome in our home. I had even bought her the food Michael told us she eats and her own bowls.

Having our small family here was a joy, even in the face of the tragedy we all had endured.

The night before Brian's celebration of life, we had Simone, Gina, Joe, Joey, Charles, and Jim's brother and family come by for dinner. Jim's brother Andy could not make the celebration due to getting his daughter, Olivia, back to school after spring break. Gina and Joe offered to pick up Brian's ashes for us since they were close to the crematory. My heart went out to Simone that evening. She was so lost and sad. I just wanted to hug her and tell her it was all going to be fine, but I could not tell her that. Grief is personal and takes time to heal after what the three of us had been through and experienced. There was no cure; only time was our healer and the wonderful memories that Brian left behind.

Sunday was here, which was Brian's 34th birthday and the celebration of his amazing life! As I was getting ready, so many thoughts were swirling in my head: how had we arrived at this time and place in our lives? Was this all part of our soul growth? Had I made a contract with my soul to lose a child in this lifetime? What about Jim and Michael? Were we all connected to this event in our lives? So many questions. I had to know the answers.

Michael and Quinnia picked up the cake and took Lady with them. I had picked up the plants the day before because the florist was closed on Sunday. All our guests would be arriving around 11:30 a.m. or so, and Pastor Phil would start around 12:30 p.m. with the program. We had ordered Mexican food; we had Patti's blessing on that because that was also served at Tommy's celebration.

We had a picture of Brian to place at the front in the reception hall and a guest book. It was a picture of Brian at Christmas dinner in 2014 when he had come to visit us. He was so happy and loved Larsen's restaurant and the food. I even remember what he ate that night. How can I forget?

Jim and I placed the plants on the tables. Suddenly, I remembered that our son was born on a Sunday. I started to cry and called Jim over and told him. We both hugged and cried, our moment before all the guests were to arrive.

It was a beautiful day and one I know Brian and Tommy were smiling down upon. The celebration was truly heartwarming.

This is the celebration of life program from that day of remembrance and healing:

A Celebration of the Life of Brian Anthony Dubrasky

Born March 18, 1984. Of course he woke up at Midnight ready to party. A mere 15-1/2 hours of labor later he burst on the scene quite loudly.

33 event-filled years later he passed from this world the morning of February 15, 2018.

No mourners/no funeral: "The measure of a man is not how he died but how he lived" —Brian's eulogy for his good friend Drew who passed in September, 2017. Brian's ashes will be scattered by friends and family at the places he loved.

Brian is survived by his parents, Janet & Jim, brother Michael and sister-in-law Quinnia. By the love of his Life, Simone, and her parents, Gina & Joe.

Brian had a host of extended family living in the US, England, and Australia. He loved his grandparents, & his cousin Jesse; who had passed on before him, as had many good friends among whom his fellow wanderer, Tommy.

They travel on ahead of us.

Menu:
11:30 to 12:00 'Happy Hour' in the Bar

12:00 to 12:30 Food & Conversation with Friends and Families

12:30 An overview of a Life by Pastor Phil

Brian's Thanksgiving, 2017, letter read by Pastor Phil

What Brian Taught Me, By Simone

Remembering a Life by some of those who were closest (His brother, Michael, friends; Brandon, Charles, Danny, Matt, & Ryan)

Video Montage—A Huge Thank You to Charles

Open Mic for those who want to share a remembrance about Brian

2:00 Conclusion

SCHOOLS: Pinecrest Pre and Kindergarten School, St. John de la Salle Elementary, Stevenson Ranch Elementary, La Mesa Jr High, Valencia SHS, Hart SHS, COC, CSUN

OCCUPATIONS: Carpenter, Personal Trainer, Emergency Medical Technician, Waiter, Bartender, Bouncer, Stand-Up Comic, Graphic Novel Writer/Illustrator, Dog Walker

COMPETITIVE SPORTS: Boxing (Golden Gloves), Mixed Martial Arts (amateur)

ACTIVITIES: Running, Hiking, Weight Lifting, skateboarding, snowboarding, wake boarding, cliff jumping, skydiving, snorkeling, scuba diving, para-sailing, jet skiing, and mountain biking

ENJOYMENTS: Piano, guitar, reading, drawing, painting, and cooking (all self-taught, of course)

LANGUAGES: English, Spanish, Portuguese (worked at a bar in Lagos, Portugal), German, Italian, French, Studying Russian, Mandarin, Japanese prior to his passing

FAVORITE PLACES in CALIFORNIA: San Diego, Yosemite, Santa Clarita, Solvang, Santa Barbara, Santa Monica, San Francisco, Lake Tahoe, Big Bear, Monterey/Carmel, Mount Shasta

STATES EXPLORED: Alaska, Arizona, Colorado, Connecticut, Hawaii, Nevada, New York, Oregon, Utah, Washington, Wyoming

COUNTRIES EXPLORED (with no money, of course): Austria, Croatia, Czech Republic, England, France, Germany, Portugal, Slovakia, Slovenia, Spain, Switzerland, Italy, Poland, Hungary, The Netherlands, and Mexico

Brian said that his favorite place in Europe was Innsbruck, Austria…to just stand and look out at the beautiful and marvelous scenery…

MEMORABLE SAYINGS:
"Check it out…"
"The service industry seems to produce comedians."

Jim also wrote the Life of Brian that Pastor Phil read aloud:

Brian Anthony Dubrasky

Brian was born at 3:15 pm on March 18, 1984 after a mere 15 ½ hours of labor, he was taken by emergency c-section at Santa Monica Hospital. He was the only baby born on that Sunday and had all the attention of the nurses in the nursery.

Brian was only an infant for a very short time. He had so much to do and at 3 months he grabbed the bottle from his mother's hand and started drinking it. He never really crawled; he stood up at 7 months and promptly ran across the living room until he fell. Got up and ran across again. By the end of the day he could run without falling.

He was always ready for new adventures and loved waking up to see what that day had in store. We called him "Mr. Rambunctious" as he never sat still and was into everything!

His brother, Michael was born 12 months and 3 weeks after him. Brian was a good brother and loved Michael so much, he called him "Miggles" and Michael called Brian "Bri-man." They had such fun together growing up and being best buds. Brian's friends became Michael's and Michael's Brian's.

Brian loved going to visit his grandparents in North Hollywood and his Nana and Pop Pop in Las Vegas. He loved his cousin, Jesse who was five years older than he.

Jesse would visit us in the summers and we all have fond memories of going to the beach, movies, playing games, eating out and just hanging around.

When he got his first bike he was irate that we'd left the training wheels on. So his father took them off. He'd pedal once or twice then fall over. Then three or four times and fall over. He was ready to cry but wouldn't. Just gritted his teeth and climbed back on. By the end of an hour he stopped falling over.

We're grateful we never saw his skateboarding.

We always had a bunch of their friends over for sleepovers. If Michael was not invited to a sleep over Brian always asked if his brother could come. Thus began a beautiful friendship with Joey Chung and his family during kindergarten and all the way to adulthood.

Brian attended St John De La Salle from 1st grade to 4th. In 1994 after the earthquake The Chungs moved, but

Brian and Joey still stayed in touch and met for weekend sleepovers at their place or ours.

Brian was always ready to learn. He woke up with a smile on his face, loved going to school and always did his homework before he went out to play. He played soccer and was in cub scouts with Dad as a leader.

When it was obvious that the neighborhood had a 'fight club' like the movie, Brian's dad took him to get boxing lessons figuring that would get it out of his system. The coaches watched Brian and recruited him for Golden Gloves.

His friends among them (Tommy, Brandon & Ryan) and their beautiful sister Kylie (whom Brian adored and loved as a little sister) and friends like Danny, Matt, Brad, Charles and many others were in and out of each others' homes, opening every refrigerator and helping themselves.

We had the opportunity to visit our dear friends, Cindi & Bill in Denver, Colorado (1994) when they lived there and when they moved to Anchorage, Alaska in 1999. Great memories of panning for gold, fishing, seeing a moose in the neighborhood, bears, and eagles and seeing the incredible glaciers.

For ten years after high school, Brian moved in and out of our home living with friends then returning. He and Tommy visited Europe twice, and even worked in Lagos, Portugal for 6 weeks and loved it!

Apparently, there were many great parties at our house while we were on vacation or out of the country. So we've been told by neighbors and his friends.

In 2012 Brian moved to San Diego and made a new life for himself. Made new friends and had a family life with Simone and her family; Gina, Joe and little Joey; her much younger brother.

Our last family vacation together was Thanksgiving 2016 in Hawaii. We are so grateful we had that beautiful time together as a family.

Now, our beloved son is gone; gone way too soon. We grieve for the tomorrows we'll never share and the conversations we'll never have.

But Brian would say that grief doesn't honor what he valued:

He had always lived fully and in the present. He hadn't postponed any part of his life. Hadn't wasted a single day at any job he didn't want to do just to make money for security or prestige or to obtain some status symbol.

Brian passed on at half his father's age but did twice as much, saw more of the world, learned to do more things, affected more lives positively.

Brian loved sharing a meal with family and friends as much as he loved raiding a refrigerator. Always ate with gusto never settling for a mediocre meal.

He never hesitated to help a friend.

Never chose purchasing a possession over spending money on having an experience.

Whatever he did it was because he chose to do it. He did it whole heartedly and with as little help from others as possible. He would rather learn by making the mistakes himself. He always accepted the sometimes disastrous results. But Brian would keep at something until he mastered it.

Always up for an adventure—no pre-planning necessary. Calculating risk just ruined the fun. As parents we are glad we didn't know the half of it.

We are grateful for the years he had in San Diego with Simone, who was the love of his life and whom he intended to marry. You can just see how happy they were in the photos.

Perhaps because he was born of a code blue emergency C-section, Brian had an inherent understanding that we are all living on borrowed time. So he never wasted a moment of his time and just lived and squeezed all he could out of whatever time he had.

We came across this by the cartoonist, Stephan Pastis and it has given us some comfort:

> "Nobody knows what we're doing here. Some have faith that they do but no one knows. So we are scared. We are alone. And we end. And we don't know where we go. So we cling to money for comfort. And we chase awards for immortality. And we hide in the routine of our days.
>
> "…*So love everyone you're with. Because comforting each other on this journey we neither asked for nor understand is the best we can do.*"
>
> And laugh as much as you can.
>
> —Stephan Pastis

Sitting there while the pastor was reading what Jim wrote was extremely hard for both of us. But it had to be done. We wanted everybody to know how very special our son was. After that, he read Brian's meditations and reflections from Thanksgiving. I tried to hear Brian saying it.

Next up were Simone, Michael, and the five of Brian's friends. Simone could barely contain herself; she was so distraught at losing her boyfriend and best friend. Michael's was short, as he did not like speaking in public, but he did a tribute to the brother he grew up with. Ryan and Brandon, the brothers, spoke next. Tears were streaming down

Brandon's face; they did a wonderful tribute to their best friend. Danny and Matt had so much to share, things none of us knew. Charles's speech was short and sweet; he spoke of Casper missing Brian and always looking for him. What broke my heart was that poor dog loved Brian so much. Brian was the alpha male, and that dog followed him and I know enjoyed their hikes, beach walks, and all the car rides he took with his master. How long would Casper live, missing Brian and wondering why he never came back to pick him up?

Pastor Phil opened up the microphone, and Patti spoke of our beloved Brian and how much they missed him dropping by. I could not speak or get up. I was sitting there like stone listening to everybody speak about my son. Jim was constantly holding my hand and rubbing my back.

Out of nowhere, Joey appeared. Oh my god! I had no way of getting in touch with Joey, but his brother Rory was on Facebook and knew about Brian's passing. He did Messenger me that they would be there. I was elated that Joey and his mom and dad showed up. Joey spoke about how he and Brian met in kindergarten and about their friendship through the years, and how much he loved eating "American" food at our house—most especially spaghetti. Afterward, I jumped up and hugged him. His mom and dad came over to talk to us.

At this time, Charles had put the montage on for everybody to see. I never truly got to see it because we were busy chatting with the Chungs. I did see it when Charles had finished it. He did a remarkable tribute for his friend, and I know Brian would have been honored.

After the montage, we cut the cake and served it to our guests. We had around eighty attendees, and we were pleased it went well.

As we slowly thanked our guests for joining us, I felt such a sense of loss. It was like, What am I supposed to do now? We gathered up what was left of the cake and asked the workers to please take some. We gave all the plants away and flowers that were brought by. It was time to go home and spend time with Michael and Quinnia before they had to go back to Portland.

After Michael and Quinnia left, it was just Jim and I again. I still had a lot of Brian's clothes to go through but did want Joey to come by and get a few T-shirts. He promised he would come by in the next week or so.

Jim and I made a decision to go see Uncle Brian and spread some of Brian's ashes as per his wishes in Australia. Our travel agent made the arrangements for us, and I called my cousin to inform her when we would be there.

At the end of March, Joey came to visit us and brought us a lovely homemade meal of his "famous" carnitas. It was so good to see him and catch up on his life. I was so grateful he and his parents came to the celebration.

During this time, because of Stacey, we met a lovely woman, Lynn, who dropped off meals for us. We have since become great friends, and I shall cherish her always. Turns out, her son's name is Brian.

Chapter Ten

April–May 2018

We were leaving the last week of April, first to Melbourne for a few days and then off to South Australia to spend a week with my uncle and cousin. We had packing to do and needed to obtain some of Tommy's ashes from Patti, so we could spread his and Brian's together. We were very careful how we packed them in the suitcases.

Before we left, we met Danny and Carly to turn over the car to them. They graciously took us to lunch afterward and drove off with the car. I knew in my heart that Brian was very happy his friend was driving his BMW, even if it was a 2005.

I donated the rest of Brian's clothes to a homeless shelter. Joey had picked out a few T-shirts of Brian's. He loved his "bro" so much, as he called him. They had been friends for almost thirty years.

Jim and I were looking forward to Australia, not the long flight mind you, but seeing Uncle Brian and my cousin Sharmain. We were lucky we had the means to make this trip and see my uncle before he left this world.

Melbourne is a fascinating city, with the river Yarra going through it and the many cultures, all getting along.

You don't hear of mass shootings and murders in this huge country. The Australians are friendly people with huge hearts. Melbourne is very diverse in culture, cuisine, and art.

We stayed on the Yarra at the Langham, one of our favorite hotels. We were given a room with a fabulous view of the city skyline and river. We slept for over ten hours our first night. We needed these few days to rest up before seeing my uncle and cousin. Once we woke up and had breakfast, we took a walk along the river. It was their fall and our spring, so there was a little chill in the air, although it was very pleasant.

We were strolling along, and I looked down, and there right in front of me was a beautiful white feather. Jim and I looked at each other and both said, "Brian." I could feel our son was with us, and I know Jim felt it as well. I picked up the feather and put it in my pocket. We had sat so long on the plane that we walked further down and then decided to sit for a while to enjoy the view. The bench we sat on had a slat missing, but the one next to us did not. A lady was having her lunch and was sitting in the middle of the bench—so no room for us until she left.

Finally, she got up and left. We waited, and I tried not to be too anxious, as I was ready to sit down. There, where the lady had been sitting, was a perfect white feather. Again? Two in a row? It was our Brian telling us he was with us; I believe that with my whole heart and soul.

After a few days of rest, it was time to head for our plane to Adelaide, where we would meet up with my cousin. We rented a car so she could drive us around the following week, since neither Jim nor I were comfortable with the "wrong side of the road." It was so lovely seeing her again and having her stay at the hotel, just down the hall from us. She had taken a few weeks off work to spend time with us and her father.

This time was so different from the last time. We were spending a whole week in a small town in the southern territory. Jim and I were used to the big city and that way of life. This was much slower paced, and the streets really do roll up at 8:00 at night. There was no ambient light from the city out there; it was dark and with a full moon that lit up the sky.

The hotel was just being built the last time we were there. It was luxurious compared to the cabin we stayed in last time. It was quite lovely and very roomy. Sharmain was impressed, as she had not been inside.

She dropped us off to check in and settle ourselves and would be back in a few hours. After we unpacked, I needed to walk after sitting for so long. Port Pirie, being a small town, consisted of a main street and a few side streets with housing behind. We walked the length of the main street and immediately noticed all the bird feathers all over the ground, although neither of us saw any birds. These were all white feathers; it was truly an amazing site. I picked a few up, and Jim and I looked at each other and both said, "Our Brian."

After our walk, true to her word, Sharmain came to take us to see my beloved uncle. Bless his heart, he had really aged since a few short years ago. He was coughing a lot and could barely walk. Sharmain had rented a wheelchair for him while we were there. We wanted to take him out to see the countryside with us and to get his favorite meat pies at the Stone Hut, outside of the town of Laura. It was a lovely drive, and my uncle was in good spirits, singing and telling jokes. We got him a few pies to take home and warm up later for his tea.

On the way back from Laura, Sharmain stopped the car and told Jim and I to look up at the sun; there was a huge circle around the sun, quite a phenomenal site and of the likes we had never seen. It was a bit eerie. Jim and I took pictures and were in awe of it. It was like a halo around the sun. We would look it up later at the hotel to see what caused such an amazing site. It turns out the ring is caused by sunlight passing through ice crystals in cirrus clouds within the earth's atmosphere. It was truly an amazing site and one I will never forget. I am sure Brian was somehow giving us a sign?

Jim and I did want to see the Indian Ocean and spread some of Brian's and Tommy's ashes. Sharmain mentioned a lovely place that was about an hour's drive to the coast. We could get lunch and take our time driving back and seeing some of the small towns along the way. We needed to give Uncle Brian a rest in between, after going to Laura.

After giving our dear uncle a rest, Sharmain took us to Moonta Bay at the end of the inlet from Port Pirie. It was a drive, but a lovely drive, and our uncle was again in good spirits. He held my hand in the back seat and told me how happy he was that we were there to see him again. I tried to hide my tears and could see Sharmain give me a look from the rearview mirror. She was, as she said it "over the moon" to see us again.

Moonta Bay was absolutely beautiful, with a long fishing pier. There were hardly any people around; it was very quiet since it was their fall. Sharmain and Uncle Brian sat on a bench while Jim and I went out on the pier to spread the ashes. It was a bit chilly but so very refreshing. We were almost at the bottom of the earth, or so it seemed. We wished our son and Tommy well in their adventures beyond as we spread the ashes in the ocean. Tears streaming down our faces, we could not believe we were here at this point in our lives.

Afterward, we ate fish and chips at a lovely restaurant right on the water. We were creating memories to last the rest of our lives with family in Australia. How lucky were we?

Sharmain stopped to get us some ice cream sundaes from McDonald's; we sat in the park under a tree and ate our sundaes. It was so amazing being here and enjoying a simple sundae with our uncle and cousin. Almost three months since our son passed, and here we were in South Australia. So much had happened in a short time, but yet it seemed a lifetime ago that our son passed on that cool day in San Diego. I could still see his feet on the pavement, his body covered in a yellow tarp. That always set me off—tears and sadness would overtake me. Jim knew what I was feeling, but I don't think anybody else could. Jim and I shared a bond that was hard to explain. We were grieving parents, a mother and father who loved their firstborn so much and felt such a tremendous loss.

Sharmain promised to find us a place among the trees to spread some more of the ashes. Just before it was time to leave, she took us with Uncle Brian to a place called Wirrabara. It was an area with lots of trees and a hiking path. When we stopped, it was exactly what we were looking for. Brian loved hiking and trees. I knew he and Tommy would be pleased with the area. It was cold and a bit rainy that day, so Sharmain and our uncle stayed in the car.

Jim and I had the ashes and walked onto the path; it smelled so good, like a forest. It was damp and very cold. I wanted the perfect spot for Brian and Tommy. Jim did not want me to go far, and finally I stopped and said, "Here." We both said our words to our son and his best friend. It was bittersweet.

We thanked Sharmain for all she had done for us. The next day, she drove us back to Adelaide to catch our flight to Melbourne. Saying a final goodbye to Uncle Brian was not easy. This time we knew we would never see him again. He promised to give our Brian a huge hug when he arrived in heaven, as well as to my mom and the rest of the family that had passed over.

On the drive back to Adelaide, it was dreary and rainy. Sharmain was a very good driver and concentrated on the road. I was enjoying the clouds and the rain, when all of a sudden I saw the most beautiful rainbow in the distance and looked in awe. I felt warm inside as if I was immersed in a cocoon of peace and love. It was a feeling that words cannot even begin to describe, but it felt wonderful. Brian? I believe so.

Saying goodbye is never easy. My cousin and I held onto each other crying. We had only met for the first time a few short years ago, but we had grown close through texting and phone calls. We were definitely family and more than cousins; we were sisters at heart.

We flew back to Melbourne for another week to explore more areas to spread the ashes before heading home.

During the week in Melbourne, we both felt a bit better. We were so grateful we had the opportunity to see my family again. I wanted to see the Twelve Apostles, although technically there are only eight left. The rapid rate of erosion, unfortunately, will reduce them even further in the near future. Jim wanted to see a real steam train and ride it through the countryside to a sanctuary and a vineyard.

We did both and spread the ashes in a place called Selby on the way to the train. Again, it was a hiking trail that we knew the boys would love. After we did that, we found not one but two white feathers: Brian and Tommy giving us their blessings.

The day before we left for home, we took a bus to the Twelve Apostles on the Great Ocean Road. It was cold and rainy, but still we had booked it and wanted to see the rugged coast where the Apostles were located in Port Campbell National Park. I wanted to spread the ashes in the Tasman Sea if at all possible.

It was a long trip but very pleasant on the Great Ocean Road. We wished we had more time to explore this beautiful country. There is so much to see and do. "Another time," we both said to each other.

When we arrived at the Twelve Apostles, it was really cold, rainy, and windy. That did not deter us; we walked to the edge of a cliff and took out the packets of the last remaining ashes we had brought. After we spread the last ashes, not one but two rays of sunshine appeared in the distance out of a dense cloud. We took a picture so as not to forget that magnificent sight. Yes, both Brian and Tommy were telling us how pleased they were! This was not our imaginations but the boys letting us know we did good!

It was a long flight home but well worth it. We made so many lovely memories, and had pictures to show for it.

Walking into our bedroom after arriving home, I noticed a few things were off. One of my pictures hanging on the wall was very crooked. None of the others were, but what really startled me was that my jewelry box was in the wrong place. I asked Jim if he had moved it, and he said "no." What the heck? Was it my imagination? Had someone been in our house? I checked everything, and nothing else was askew or missing.

We arrived home a few days before my birthday, which was May 19th. I so desperately wanted a reading with a medium and had scheduled one with Tim Braun for May 30th. I had met him before, in 2016. Patti told me she had seen him a few months after Tommy passed, and that he was talented. I had read his book *Life and Death* while on our trip, and it really helped me with my grief and knowing our son's journey after he passed. I was so looking forward to his reading.

I had also started reading some books by Patrick Mathews, another medium who had written several books. The first one I read was *Never Say Goodbye*, which really gave me insight into our souls and grief. There is a section on losing a child and even one on suicide. I found this book to be so helpful in the grieving process. I had to book an appointment with him as well, so I did, but due to his busy schedule, I could not get one until December 5th. I felt he was worth the wait!

In the meantime, I was anxious to speak to Tim to find out what he had to say.

On my birthday, I was busy cleaning my closet. I bent over to get a shirt that had fallen, and there on the floor was a dime. I picked it up and looked at the date, 2004. That was the year my mother passed. Too many coincidences with the penny, feathers, rainbows, and items being moved. I knew in my heart this dime was from my mother, wishing me a happy birthday. For some reason, I felt Brian was showing her how it's done after you pass over to the other side.

On the 26th, we had a few of Brian's friends over for a barbecue to thank them all for their support: Patti, Mark,

Audrey, Ryan, Krystle, Danny, and Carly. Ryan and Krystle brought their little girl, Scarlett, who was adorable. Brian was one of the groomsmen at both Danny and Carly's wedding and Ryan and Krystle's.

I was cleaning the patio table, as it was dusty from being outside. I have a planter on the table and removed it to water the plants inside to spruce up the place. Being a bit of a perfectionist, I had to make sure everything was just right.

The next morning, before the guests arrived, I took one last look around to make sure it was perfect. For some reason I picked up the planter, don't know why, but underneath was a shiny penny. I cried and thanked my son. I knew he was there and would be while his friends were with us. It was another way he was telling me he was around.

Suffice to say, it was a wonderful barbecue and so nice to have friends of Brian's around us.

Chapter Eleven
Reading with Tim Braun

I was so excited, my reading appointment with Tim Braun was at 11:00 a.m. that day. Tim started by explaining how he does his reading: he does not ask you questions; he tells you what he sees and explains to the best of his ability.

Mother is on the left side, and my father in on the right.

There were three to five souls behind my mother, and one was my son. My father started saying he wished he had been closer to me and wraps his arms around me. He was proud of me and loved me. He was helping me the past weeks and months with an energy push.

My son came through, wrapping his arms around me so tightly with a thumbs-up. He looked older than his thirty-three years but was healthy now. His heart was strong and all off his chest now that he had arrived. He had concealed so much from me; he was a good actor and had so much emotional baggage prior to passing. He regrets hurting me and was sorry for the separation we had prior to his passing. He kept a lot to himself. At this time, my dad, his grandfather, places his right arm on Brian's shoulder; there is tremendous respect with each other, and they both smile.

He explained he is busier than ever over there and misses all of us. He mentions a little boy, Joey, and gives a thumbs-up again. Brian could not control his excitement at being in heaven. He had moved up a level due to his helping friends and being kind and nice; he was well-liked and successful. There were so many people affected by his life. He arrived to a fabulous destination and was very happy.

Brian adored his grandmothers and was with them as well. Brian was petting a large dog—very happy the dog was there with him in heaven.

I cried when he mentioned my son was with him in the reading. I knew Brian had concealed a lot when we spoke while he was in jail. He had his own demons; he wanted to protect me from all that. He did not and could not share those with his mother.

My dad and I were not close—it was true—but I knew he respected that my mom and I were. He had his faults, as we all do. I know now he did the best he could while he was here.

Yes, Brian adored his grandmothers. He loved them so much!

Brian being with a dog brought joy to my heart. Lola was with him; he loved her so and did not know she was put down while he was in jail. I never told him; I did not have the heart to tell him. They are together in spirit.

I felt so much better after our reading. Tim helped me put all that Brian had gone through into perspective. It was his journey he had to follow, even though we were all connected in this life, and he chose to be my son. I also had to endure the pain of losing him. We will meet again when it is my time to pass over. I have my journey to complete to fruition, and losing my son is part of that journey.

Chapter Twelve

June–November 2018

My cousin Jill wanted to visit LA. She came at the end of May for two weeks. It was lovely to have my English cousin and show her our home and where we live. She was a joy to be with, and seeing our home in her eyes was joyful. We had only met the first time a year ago.

We took her to the Getty Museum on Pacific Coast Highway, to which I had never been. Jim had been before we met and was excited to go with me and my cousin. It was lovely and a nice day in Malibu. Afterward, we took Jill to Gladstone's, which brought back memories of taking our sons there before Michael joined the Navy. Afterward, we drove up the coast and showed her Malibu Colony and where a lot of the movie stars lived. It was quite a day and one filled with memories and pictures.

I took her to Ventura one day to show her that part of California. She was amazed at the homes on the beach in Oxnard. She took lots of pictures, and we ate at Brophy Bros., one of my favorite restaurants in Ventura in the marina. It was a truly marvelous day; Jill and I were forming a special bond.

We took her to Vegas to see my sister Gail and my Aunt Barbara's family. My aunt had passed away of cancer after a fifteen-year battle in 2011. Jim and I did not care for Vegas, especially after losing my mom, nephew, and dad. It was not the same for us anymore. Jill had to see the rest of the family, and it was good to see my sister, especially after my baby sister, Cindy, had passed the year before.

After Vegas and before Jill left, I took her to Beverly Hills and of course the Hollywood Mann's Chinese Theatre and the Hollywood Walk of Fame. She took many photos and kept saying how excited she was to actually be in Hollywood. I took her to my favorite restaurant in Beverly Hills, La Scala, for a chopped salad. Afterward, we walked around and finally ended up at the Beverly Wilshire Hotel for drinks and people watching.

I could not drink since I was driving, but Jill enjoyed sitting at the bar and looking around. I knew she was hoping to see a "movie star," but alas we did not.

All too soon, it was time for my beautiful cousin to leave and go back to Manchester, England. She had immensely enjoyed her holiday, and we told her she was welcome anytime.

A few days after Jill left, Jim and I were sitting at the pool and just enjoying the June weather. It was not too hot, quite pleasant. I was sitting up and was watching a dandelion puff float around me and before me. All of a sudden it became a wing and disappeared as if it went into an opening of some kind. I remembered saying, "Jim, did you see that?" He said, "What?" I was in awe and could not say what I saw. I can still see it in my mind to this day. It was something I will never forget. I now understand the "veil" between here and heaven. I have read it's only a thin veil, and I truly understand what that means.

Every night before I would fall asleep, I asked my Brian to come visit me during the night. I would talk to him and ask him to please tell me what really happened with him. I remember so vividly trying to fall asleep, and I saw my beautiful handsome son before me: he was on the path in Australia where we spread his and Tommy's ashes. He was so handsome and wearing a bright checkered shirt with all the colors of a rainbow. He never wore bright colors—only black, brown, or navy. This was actually a shirt I bought for Jim in Santa Fe years ago. Brian was smiling at me and so happy. He did not speak, but I knew he was enfolded in love and was at peace. I blinked, and he was gone. I tried to bring him back, to no avail. He only gave me a glimpse.

The rest of the summer was quite unique. I had woken up one morning in late June with a detached retina. Having emergency surgery was not fun, but having had a detached retina before in my right eye, I knew what to expect.

We had planned on visiting Michael and Quinnia in early August. I could fly, as the retina appeared to be OK after the surgery in June. Jim and I love flying and were excited about seeing our youngest. Michael and Quinnia, with Lady in the car, took us to Long Beach, Washington and to Astoria, Oregon. We were in awe of the greenery and beauty of the Pacific Northwest. Halfway through the trip, my left eye retina started becoming detached again. My doctor had warned me, and I told Michael and Jim. We had to fly back as soon as possible. This time, the surgeon would have to place a band behind the eye to secure the retina in place. I would have a gas bubble in my eye for several months. Ugh!

Before we left, Michael told me what happened to him after he learned Brian had passed on. He went outside that night to have a smoke. He lives across the street from a small, wooded area—nothing there but trees. As he was standing there thinking of his brother and their childhood, he saw a light appear. It was a strange light, sort of like a flashlight but different; he really could not explain it. He wanted to go investigate, but it was late, and he had to get up for work in the morning.

What really stopped him was that the light flashed at him and then was gone; it went upward toward the sky. He told me he felt it was Brian telling him he was OK.

I swear Brian was holding my hand before surgery. I could feel his presence with me and knew all was going to be fine. I remember asking him to be with me and stay with me during this very scary surgery. I had faith in my doctor, but still, anything could go wrong. I remember starting to cry before they took me in the operating room. Once in there, it was cold, and my head had to be way back on the table. Maybe it was the drugs, but I felt a peace overcome me as I drifted off to the abyss. When I came to, Brian was my first thought. My baby was with me, and then the doctor came and said surgery was a huge success!

Upon our arrival home after my surgery, Jim was opening the door and smelled gas. I did not, but he went into the kitchen. One of the gas burners was on full blast. Neither of us had been in the kitchen prior to leaving early that morning for my surgery. Jim dropped me off and then went to eat. Brian, again, was letting us know he was here. Jim said it could not have been on long.

By mid-August, I so needed a reading from a medium. My reading with Patrick was not until December. I searched the internet and found Kirstin Ross at Forever in Spirit. She was close by and highly rated; she also did phone readings. I called her and loved her voice. We booked an appointment.

When Kirstin called, she mentioned that my son had passed over and was with me. He had been with me during my surgery. He was helping me heal. She also mentioned a trip we took, and he was with us on that trip. He loved the places we spread his ashes. An initial T and D were with him. She mentioned rainbows and that Brian was studying with the best artists and mentioned Van Gogh. He is happy and in a great place, and I should not worry. She saw what she thought was a pit bull with him. He had no pain when we passed. He woke up floating. We will see each other in eternity.

I was amazed and cried with happiness and joy. Although I will always miss Brian's presence here, I felt he was in a good place. All she said was true: T was for Tommy and D for Drew. It was interesting that she mentioned Van Gogh. I have a huge version of *Le café de nuit* in my office. Brian studying with the best made me happy; he was such an artist while on earth. Again, there was confirmation that Lola was with my beloved son.

My cousin Tosh was coming with Michelle at the beginning of October and would stay with us for a week. They would rent a car and visit the places they wanted to see. I was homebound due to the gas bubble, as it would take at least two months after the surgery for it to dissolve. I let Tosh know that they were welcome to do whatever they wanted, and perhaps before they left we could take them out to a restaurant.

Tosh and Michelle were busy. They were gone all day and would arrive late at night. They had so much to see and do on their bucket list. We were happy they could get around on their own. They started calling us their "Hollywood parents." We loved it and were happy they were here. It was nice having family around. The week went fast, and off they went to San Francisco and then Vegas before returning to England.

I went into the guest room to strip the sheets and noticed a 20 pence coin where Michelle's suitcase had been. Brian had been visiting with his cousin as well. How beautiful: although we could not see him, he was with us. My spirit soared, and I thanked him for being with us.

In early November, we had scheduled a trip to Kauai to spread some more ashes for Brian. He had never been to the island of Kauai; it was my favorite, and we asked Patti for some of Tommy's ashes. Just before we were to leave, I found out my sister Gail was in the hospital. I would never forgive myself if I went on our trip without seeing her. I knew she had COPD and was diabetic. Jim understood and offered to go with me. It was easier to drive, so we did. I told my sister Diane that we were going to see Gail. Diane asked for a full report, as she was concerned as well. Out of six of us, there were only three of us left.

Gail was so thin and I could tell very ill. She was to be released the next day, and I told her we would stay and take her home. She was happy to see us. I mentioned to Jim that when we got back from Hawaii, I should come get her and bring her home to stay with us. Jim, as always, was a real trooper and agreed.

I took Jim back to the hotel and went to stay with Gail until visiting hours were over. We had a good talk that night, and I am so very happy we did. We laughed and cried, but mostly we held each other. She was feeling better and mentioned how sad it was that Mom, me, and she had all lost children. She told me that she would never forget all we did for Jesse: Jim was a good uncle to him, and he always told her how much fun he had at our house during his summer vacations. I told her it was our pleasure and that Brian and Michael loved him so much. He was their older brother in so many ways.

The next day, she was released. She wanted a hamburger, so we took her out and then home and made sure she had her medication. Jim and I walked to her pharmacy, which was next to her apartment. I cried on the way and thanked Jim for coming with me. He could have stayed home, but he wanted to make sure I was all right. I remember thanking God for bringing Jim to me.

We arrived home and got packed for our trip. Seven days in paradise was just what the doctor ordered. My eye was better; the gas bubble had dissolved. Although I could not see well in the left eye, I was so grateful for the nearly perfect vision in my right. At this point, I was pretty sure I was overcompensating with the right eye.

I always felt lighter in Hawaii. I felt something in my soul whenever we visited the islands. I loved the Hawaiians and their aloha spirit. We were booked at the Grand Hyatt in Poipu, which is absolutely a beautiful hotel with pools all over and a gorgeous beach. It was just what we needed to rest our weary souls. Our first night, we rested and watched the color-filled sky at sunset. Brian was always in my thoughts, and I could not help but wonder if he had anything to do with painting the sky. I was in awe and sat for a long time on the balcony and watched the sun go down and then the stars come out. It was a glorious night filled with so many stars—no ambient light to mar the amazing sight. I could hear the ocean in the distant, waves crashing on the shore, and felt the peace in my heart.

After going to the islands for so many years, we had pretty much seen it all. I only wanted to spread the ashes in the ocean and in Waimea Canyon, also known as the Grand Canyon of the Pacific. Otherwise, I wanted to read and lie by the gorgeous saltwater pools at the hotel.

I texted Gail some photos and asked how she was doing and feeling. She texted back for us to enjoy our trip and thanked us for coming to see her. I was not sure she was telling me the truth, but I knew I would go see her once we got home.

Jim drove to Waimea Canyon after we felt rested and ready for the drive. It was gorgeous going up the canyon; it had rained and was slow going. The rain did not deter us, as we knew it would be sunny later. It was cool once you get up to the lookout. We had both Brian's and Tommy's ashes in our pockets and needed to find a place without people around. We walked around, and as we did, I looked down and saw not one but two feathers. I picked them up and showed Jim. He looked, and there weren't any others around. A sign? Both boys were letting us know they were happy.

We found a perfect spot overlooking the intensely colorful canyon. It was like heaven on earth. I wished I could fly around and go into the waterfalls. I knew that is exactly what Brian and Tommy were doing. I was a bit envious that they could do that now, being in spirit. I wanted to be there. I envisioned flying through those falls and going upward into the clouds and then down again. It was an amazing feeling of being weightless.

I drove back and mentioned to Jim that I wanted another place to spread some of the ashes. I drove and found a spot and stopped. It was just perfect; the view was magnificent. I took out the ashes and spoke words to Brian and Tommy.

Afterward, a beautiful dragonfly flew right past me. Patti had told me that after Tommy passed, dragonflies were always around her. Tommy? Of course it was. He was thanking us.

The rest of our week flew by. I was reading more of Patrick Mathews's books. *Never Say Goodbye* was the first I read, and I was so inspired that I read the other two: *Forever With You* and *Everlasting Love*. A fourth book called *Only a Thought Away* was to be released in early 2019, and I could not wait. Just before we left, we spread the remaining ashes in a little cove on the beach of the hotel. It was bittersweet for both of us. As we walked back to the hotel, I knew the boys were happy with our choices of where their ashes were spread.

After being in Hawaii for a week, it was always sad going home. I had to visit my retina specialist and see Gail to help her with obtaining Social Security disability.

Once home, I was told by my retina doctor that the scar tissue in my eye had built up, and I needed surgery to clean it up. Three surgeries in one year, ugh!

However, I have such faith that my doctor knew what he was doing, and I know he saved my sight to the best of his ability. Surgery was scheduled for early December.

Thanksgiving, my favorite holiday, arrived. Just a year before, my son was in jail, and the year before that we were in Hawaii with our family. I looked at the pictures we took of all of us together and am grateful we had that time together. So much had happened in just two short years! I was looking forward to 2019.

Gail stopped returning my calls after Thanksgiving, so off we went to Vegas to see what was going on. I was worried, and so was Diane.

Jim stayed at the hotel while I went to see Gail; her home was only a few blocks away, and I promised I would call him once there.

Upon seeing my sister, I was shocked. She was so full of pneumonia and could hardly breathe. I immediately called 911. Gail did not want me to, but I could not stand to see her suffering. She was rail thin, and it broke my heart. It seemed the ambulance was at the door in less than two minutes. They were wonderful and tried to get as much information from Gail as they could.

I called Jim and told him I was following the ambulance to University Medical Center and would let him know what was happening once I was there. I called Diane, and she was on her way from Riverside to Vegas.

Once we got to the hospital, the doctors quickly evaluated her. Her blood pressure was very low, and she was having a hard time breathing. They took a blood sample and did X-rays. Everything takes time in an emergency room, but I have to say the doctors and nurses were fabulous at keeping us informed.

It was nearing 3:00 p.m., and the doctor told us she had a collapsed lung and was full of pneumonia (which I knew after seeing my dad go through it). Diane arrived and took over staying with Gail so I could go eat. I had not eaten all day—only coffee and water.

I met Jim at the restaurant at our hotel, and all I could stomach was an omelet. I had taken one bite when Diane called and said Gail was refusing to be intubated. Diane was upset and wanted Gail to do it; I knew Gail wanted to be with her son, Jesse. I did not blame Gail, and I had to agree with her. Gail was upset that I called the ambulance, but I told her I could not see her suffer that way; the hospital was the best place. In so many words, Gail had told me she was more than ready to go "home." I understood, but Diane did not: she had not lost a child.

I got there as fast as I could, and Diane was crying. I told her to go on, and I would be there with Gail if and when it happened. I sat with Gail, and the doctor came and spoke to me quietly. They could save her, but she needed to be intubated. I told him I would not overturn what Gail wanted. She was ready to go and had suffered enough. He told me they would make her comfortable and asked if I would stay with her. Of course I would; she's my sister.

It all happened so fast. Once they gave her the shot to make her comfortable, she told me, "Thank you. I know Diane could not do it, but I know you can handle it." I brushed her hair and said to her, "You go home and be with Jesse, Mom, Dad, Cathy, Cindy, Michael, and my Brian. Please give them all a kiss for me?" She said, "You know I will."

She held my hand and squeezed it. With the other, she pointed up and took her last breath. I have to say it was beautiful! I knew she was at peace and that she was with her beloved son and all our family and our Lord.

I had to wait for the doctor to declare that she had died. It was 5:30 p.m. on Monday, November 26, 2018. I had lost my son and now my sister. I called Diane and Jim to let them know. It was a long day but a day I will never forget. I am grateful I was with Gail and knew she was busy in heaven with all our family. She was sixty-one years old and had lived a hard life. Her husband had died when Jesse was five, and then she lost her only son at twenty-seven. Jesse had passed away in November of 2006, Cindy in 2017, and now Gail—all in November.

I must admit that I was a bit envious of Gail. I wanted to see my son so badly, although I know I have to be here for Jim and Michael *and* to complete my journey. When it is my time, I will gladly go without hesitation, especially knowing what I now know after reading all the books from those wonderful mediums, Tim Braun and Patrick Mathews.

As per all our family's wishes, Gail would be cremated and her ashes would be spread on a hill overlooking Vegas. My brother was the first to be spread there and then Cathy, my mom, Jesse, Dad, Cindy, and now Gail.

Diane and I decided we would spread her ashes after the New Year, as we were all busy with the holidays. We know Gail would not mind, and I wanted some of her ashes to spread in the Pacific Ocean along with Brian's.

Chapter Thirteen

December 2018

December was upon us, and 2019 was around the corner. I had my reading scheduled with Patrick and was looking forward to it on December 5th. I had only booked a half hour.

Patrick called me and asked if he had read for me before. I said, "No."

He then told me two spirits were anxiously waiting to speak to me. He said, "Your son is here; he is good looking! He is sorry he was out of it with the meds, body was weak and his mind was off. He's in perfect health now, and he has the body he always wanted to have! Everything has a reason and purpose, so not a waste." He mentioned the love I have for my son is inside me, and Brian knew how proud I was of him. It's only a temporary situation, and I will see him again. He went on about Brian being a noisemaker who loved leaving imprints. He also wanted me to know Brian was working on coming to me in my dreams.

Next, my mother came to let me know that "God gives you only what you can handle" and to send lots of love. She mentioned turning a negative into a positive and that I know more than most. We had such a bond: same life, same soul. She wanted to send love to everybody and was proud of me.

Brian came back to say that I should put a smile on my face and he sent his love to Dad and Michael: it's just a temporary situation.

How can you not cry during a reading like this? Still, you miss your family and those who have passed over. The gift Patrick gave me lifted my spirits and my soul.

My surgery to clean up the scar tissue in my left eye was the following week. Again, I asked Brian to be there with me and keep me safe. All went well, and I knew this would be the last surgery for that eye.

My cousin in Australia, Sharmain, let me know that Uncle Brian was taking a turn for the worse and was in the hospital in Port Pirie. I wanted to talk to him, but he was having a hard time breathing, and Sharmain was preparing for his passing. He passed away on what would have been my brother Michael's sixty-sixth birthday. It was so very bittersweet that he passed away on that particular date. I knew my uncle was busy visiting his mom, dad, and sisters in heaven!

In one year, I lost my son, my sisters, and my dear uncle. I learned that there are many degrees of grief. Grief for a son is, I believe, the hardest, as it's not expected. We expect to lose our parents in our lifetime but not our child or children. But heal, we do. Little by little, the shock begins to dull, and we can laugh and smile again. We can do this when we know that the love we have never dies and only gets stronger. There is no cure for grief—you must learn to live with it and continue on with our journey in life. Those who have passed on completed their journey. Whether long or short, it was their journey and soul growth.

Chapter Fourteen

2019

To me, the New Year is always a fresh start. I love the saying "out with the old, in with the new." The year 2018 was not an easy one, having lost our beloved Brian, my sister, and then my dear uncle. I knew the one-year anniversary of Brian's death would be a sad day. I read enough books to know that. However, knowing all my family are together in spirit helps the pain in my heart.

Diane and I were to meet in Vegas toward the middle of January to spread Gail's ashes. On the way to Vegas, Jim and I stopped at the rest stop before we got into Nevada. As we got out of our car, all the windows rolled down on their own. Jim thought I did it, and I thought he did it. That had never happened before. I truly believe Brian wanted us to know he was with us and so was Gail. Even Jim was amazed at all the signs from our son.

I remembered my mother told me that when she and Dad took Michael's ashes to that hill, after they had spread his ashes, she looked down and there was a folded $5 bill. A sign from her son? She knew she had found the perfect spot. It was her and my father's wishes to be spread at the same location.

February 15th was a hard day, and that date will always

be a reminder of that fateful day in 2018. I kept thinking about seeing Brian's feet on the pavement and his body covered with a tarp. I cried most of the day and stayed in. I did not want to even go out. I wanted to mourn my son all over again. My mind knew where he is, but my heart missed his presence so very much. His smile, laughter, and jokes always filled my heart with joy. He was and will always be a special soul that walked among us. Although my son was born with poop all over him and the cord around his neck, he came to enjoy being alive. I truly believe in my heart that he was three weeks late because he was so busy negotiating his contract in heaven before he was born. (Remember that I mentioned at the beginning he was born three weeks late? That's my take on it.)

It appeared that after the first of the year, more and more signs from Brian and Gail were always within my path. I would say my uncle was also always letting me know he was happy in spirit. I envisioned him toasting us with a mug of beer. I knew they were all busy celebrating being together.

What I found really incredible were all the hearts within my path. Brian always would sign his name in a card to me with a heart shape. Several times, I would look down and see a heart shape in water. Once, I saw a heart carved in the cement. It was truly amazing that Brian could do that.

On my walks, I would look up at the sky and see a cloud shaped like a perfect feather or a bird. I would sit on a bench and think of Brian, Gail, and Uncle Brian; then three beautiful blue birds would fly past me. I would cry and thank them for letting me know. How can we not believe our loved ones are around in spirit? I wish I had been more aware when my brother, mom, and dad passed. Losing a child makes one more open to these events in life.

In April, Jim and I took Brian and Gail to Malibu to spread their ashes. It was a beautiful day, a bit windy and cool. Brian always loved Leo Carrillo Beach because of the tide pools and the rocks. Jim and I walked after we parked the car, and so many memories of bringing our boys to the beach ran in my head. I would have given anything to go back in time and be there with them again. I missed my little boys and being their whole world at one time. I was the be-all and end-all of their world. My love for them is so strong and so powerful, I would sit and cry when they were asleep at night. They were such beautiful gifts from the Almighty. How could I have ever thought at one point in my life that I did not want children? I loved being a mother to my sons. I had wished for a daughter, but when Michael was born I knew it was perfect: two sons close in age. How perfect is that?

We found the right spot in an area where there were not any people. Gail was first and then our son. It was bittersweet, and we told Gail that we had brought Jesse here many times when he spent the summers with us. Brian had lost his keys here one time when he brought friends after he started driving. Jim had to bring him the spare key. It was those memories that are forever etched in one's mind. When we got to the beach, the clock read 11:11 in the car. I will never forget seeing that. We drove north a bit to eat at Neptune's, and when we left after eating, the clock read 1:11. Our angels were with us that glorious day for sure.

In May, Jim had a knee replacement. I stayed in the waiting room of Holy Cross that morning. I was, of course, thinking of Brian and praying Jim would be all right. After the doctor came to say all was well, I went to the restroom. In the sink was a heart-shaped paper cutout. I thanked my

Brian again for his gift. He was with me while waiting for word about his father.

I am so grateful that Brian chose me as his mother. I am grateful we had almost thirty-four years with him. He was a joy from the moment he was born. I am grateful Brian had the opportunities to see the world and do all he did. He gave so much of himself to so many in his life. He made friends for life, like Joey. I am grateful he met Simone and loved her with all his heart. Although, I am sad for Simone that she lost the love of her life, at this writing she has met a wonderful man and is now enjoying a relationship again, that we are most grateful for. It was all part of her journey to experience the heartache of losing a love.

Brian planted the thought in my mind to write his story—I truly believed it was him. He left a heart-shaped rubber band on my desk. During the month it took me to write this, I cannot tell you how many times I saw these numbers on the clock: 11:11, 1:11, 2:22, 8:08, 3:33, 4:44, and 5:55. It was truly uncanny. If you look up all these angel numbers on the internet you will see what they mean. Angels are never far to help and guide you and let you know you are on the right path.

Pulling out his baby book and seeing all those moments I wrote in there was hard. All his firsts. I cried for hours. I never gave the book to him or the letters I wrote on his birthdays. I guess I was waiting for him to have his first child, to experience the joy of being a father. It was not to be for my son. His journey in life was short but not too short. He still had a life that he lived of his choosing and on his terms. Jim and I are ever so grateful for that much.

One morning, before I got out of bed and while still half asleep, I dreamed I was sitting on my sofa, and Brian came in the door wearing a brown T-shirt. He was so tall and handsome. He looked at me, and my heart leapt. I could not speak, as I was dumbfounded that he was there in the flesh. He smiled at me. I woke up with a start. He was there—I know he was. I await that magnificent day when we sit in a meadow talking about all he went through while in jail and what caused his being there. That is my dream of my son and me visiting. I see it clearly in my mind. One day.

I now call my son Angel Brian. I know he is watching out for me, his father, and his brother. The bond we all shared is not lost with his passing. It is stronger than ever now. He taught us all so much and continues to do so. I will always miss his presence, though I know in my heart he is never far. He is just beyond that veil between heaven and earth. One day, we will all be together again, and that gives me the strength to carry on and complete my journey in life.

Thank you, my darling son, for all you gave us during your time on earth. You always were an exceptional soul who gave so much of himself to others. Love, always and forever, your Mother!

CHAPTER FIFTEEN

Signs and Connections

When our loved ones pass, they are still with us in spirit. We are all energy, and energy never dies; it just changes form.

What I learned losing my beloved son is that he is still here. His memory will always live on. He can send messages via electricity. He has sent pennies from heaven and feathers, birds, dragonflies, heart imprints, and hummingbirds. If you think of your loved one, they are most likely sending you a sign that they are around.

After Brian passed, all kinds of dogs have approached me. I was always scared of dogs, especially big dogs. Casper helped me get over the fear of pit bulls. One day, I was walking several weeks after Brian passed, and a beautiful golden retriever came up to me and actually got up on his hind legs and hugged me. They know that I am grieving; they are smart souls and feel the grief. I cannot even say how many dogs have come to me and looked up at me as if to say, "I know what you are going through."

Babies, because they are such new souls, know too. I have had babies (not newborn, but at least seven to eight months old) reach out their little arms to me, and the mother will say in awe, "She has never done that with a complete stranger." It is bizarre to a lot of people who don't understand. I have even had children as old as two come up to me and smile and put out their arms to hug me.

I don't presume to have all the answers to life and death, but I know what I have experienced since losing my son. All one needs to do is open one's heart. As my mother said before she passed when I asked if she were scared of dying: "We are all afraid of the unknown." I am not afraid anymore after losing Brian. I know there is life after death. It is not really death but being reborn. Once our soul has learned what we came to learn in this life, it is time for rest and rejuvenation. It is time to be enfolded in that loving peace of calm with no worries, pain, or suffering. I will never be the same after my beautiful son jumped to his death, nor would I want to be the same. I have grown so much and know this is all part of my soul journey in this life. When it is time to leave this world, I only pray that the first face I see is my son's and then after that my mother, father, brother, sisters, and nephew. God bless to everyone on earth, and I pray for peace for us all!

Love, it is all about Love.

CHAPTER SIXTEEN

Letter to Brian, 1985

I had to share this letter I recently found in our safe. There are more from Brian's many birthdays, but this one truly illustrates what an incredible soul he was even at the age of one.

May 29, 1985

To My Dearest Son, Brian:

How do I tell a little man how much mommy loves him? At 14 months you don't understand what love is yet? Oh, you kiss me and daddy and even your little brother—but you don't understand love yet.

As I watched you run around the house this morning, I was inspired to write you and tell you about YOU at 14 months. You are so cute and absolutely adorable. You've brought such joy to my life and your dad's. You run around so fast it is hard to keep up with you. You make me happy to see you so happy. What a sense of humor you have. Always laughing, always happy! Oh, but you do have your moments. You can be so cranky, and you make me angry at times, but still...I love you more than my own life.

Everywhere I take you out people come up and say what a handsome fella you are! And then they say how happy you are. Yes, my son, you are a happy child. It makes me feel so good because I feel I've helped contribute to your happiness. Every time I dress you I tell you to look at yourself in the mirror. And you do, you even kiss yourself! I wanted you to know at an early age to always like yourself. Mommy did not have very much self-confidence at an early age, but I very much want that for you and your brother. I want you both to have all the things I did not. I want to give you so much, and only the best. You and Michael deserve the best and that you shall have, that I promise little man.

Always remember, my first born, that I will always love you now and forever and until the end of time. I only hope and pray that I will be able to watch you grow up to be that fine young man that I know you will be someday. Because I feel you will be somebody, someday, very special, just as you are to me.

Love Always and Forever and ever,
Your mommy

Chapter Seventeen

Life Changes and Thank-Yous

A t this writing, Jim and I are embarking on a new chapter of our lives. We are moving to Oregon to be closer to our Michael. With this major move, we know our Brian will continue to be with us in spirit. In fact, when we drove through Oregon after visiting our Michael in Eugene, which is where he felt we would be comfortable, we stopped in Roseburg to have lunch with a dear friend, Grace. She had recently moved back to her hometown after retiring. She was so happy to see us and "sell" us on her hometown. After driving around and making sure we got the lay of the land, so to speak, we turned a corner, and there on the side of the building was "Brian's Auto Parts and Imports." To me, it was a sign from my beloved Brian. He wants us in this beautiful town for now. I will always be grateful for his insight to lead us to this place and of course, Grace.

I do have one regret; after Brian passed, we did not donate any of his organs. Because of the shock of losing him so abruptly, it never crossed my mind until recently. It pains me that we did not help others because I know Brian would have wanted that. I can only ask for forgiveness from my beautiful son. He knows how difficult it was for us, and he continues to be around in spirit.

In closing, I wish to thank so many people who stopped by after Brian's passing and who sent flowers, gift baskets, cards, and just called to see how we were. Even to this day, you continue to check on us and make sure we are OK.

Simone, even though you lost your lover and best friend, you always found time to check on Jim and me. We will always love you and appreciate the love you gave to Brian and made his last few years on earth happy. We know you were the love of his life, even when he pushed you away due to his illness. We cannot wait to attend your wedding in the near future.

Gina, Joe, and little Joey, we love you and are so grateful you are part of our lives. Thank you for everything you did to help us with the celebration. Your phone calls and texts mean the world to us. Watching Joey grow up gives us strength and such joy. We know Brian loved him very much and continues to watch over him from heaven!

Dr. Dunn, thank you for your incredible advice and words of comfort after Brian left this world. You are the *very* best psychologist, and our family will be forever grateful for your wisdom and guidance.

Liz and Ben, since meeting you in 1986, our friendship has gone through three decades of dinners and watching our children grow. Thank you for continually checking in on us after we lost Brian.

Patti and Mark, thank you for being the first to arrive with food and to understand our grief, especially given that you went through it just a few years before. How strange that we both lost our oldest sons.

Ryan and Krystle, thank you for always checking in

and bringing food. Brian was so lucky to have such a great friend, and we know he was very happy to be part of your wedding party.

Brandon, thank you for caring so much and being a true friend and confident to Brian. He loved you and your brothers very much!

Danny, Carly, Eddie, and Krysta, your love and support still continue to bring us joy in seeing your children grow.

Charles, thank you for being there and helping with the celebration. We did not ask: you were just there and helped tremendously. Thank you!

Stacey, your gifts of books and a beautiful wind chime with Brian's name on it are a true testament to what a great friend you are. You went through your own grief in 2014 when you lost your beloved Don. Your Grubhub gift card came in so handy when I could finally eat. And the flowers that adorned our table were truly magnificent. Bless you!

Martha, thank you for always being there and listening to my crying with all Brian went through while he was sick. I treasure you and our incredible friendship. Sometimes, I feel as if we were connected in another life.

Phillipa, I so appreciate your love and friendship.

Rochelle, you came all the way to Valencia from Oregon for Brian's celebration. Not only were you a great neighbor and a dear and thoughtful friend, you were also Brian's middle school principal! Thank you!

Terri, with all the stress with your job, you took time to send a most beautiful orchid and continue to check on me. I treasure our friendship and have since we met in 2009.

Cindi, forgive me for not being able to tell you everything about Brian. It was so hard going back and forth to see him in San Diego. I could not talk to anybody about what Brian was going through; it pained me deeply and still does.

Jo, when you lost Tom, I saw your pain etched on your face every day for five years. I am so very happy and grateful you met Ray and remarried. I am so honored to have your friendship and the books you brought over after Brian passed. Seeing your granddaughters grow up has been such a joy; they are beautiful young women!

Sherri, your calls, texts and support mean the world to me.

Cheryl, thank you for always reaching out to see how I am doing and for listening to me, even after losing your sister this year. Bless you.

Therese, thank you for your kind words on energy after I told you Brian passed. It was you who told me to look for the signs. Thank you!

Lynn, thank you to a new friend brought to me through my loss. It is such a coincidence that your son's name is Brian. Truly, God brought us together, and we have Stacey to thank for being the conduit.

Sandie, thank you for all your love and kindness. You were the very first friend I made in California in 1982. We all loved your wonderful barbecues and pool parties. The boys adored you and your German Shepherds. Those were the days!

Suzanne, your loss of Roger and mine of Brian brought us together. You and I know grief in such a way that is hard to actually put into words; we just know.

To my cousin Sharmain, your support and love through all this and losing your beloved father has taught me much about the family we were born into. I am proud we are cousins, and I know my mother and your father are happy we have each other.

To my incredible family in the UK: Uncle Tony, Marie, Jill, Jordana, Dawn, Tosh, and Michelle. Bless you all for your lovely flowers and cards of comfort and love. Having you all in our lives made this so much more bearable knowing we have family in Manchester, UK.

Joey, thank you for being the light in the darkness after losing Brian. We love you as a son and are so grateful for you and your lovely family. We cannot wait to show you Oregon when you come visit.

Debbie, thank you for being a friend and standing up for me those many years ago at the BAR…and for listening to my story about Brian without judgment.

To my darling husband, Jim, I could not have gone through this without you at my side. Who knew thirty-seven years ago we would go through this gut-wrenching journey together? I am grateful we've survived this together with love and kindness.

My Michael, thank you for listening and letting me cry on your shoulder even though you were grieving the loss of your only brother and sibling. I am so grateful you and Brian had each other growing up. You never fought but always got along and supported each other. The memories your dad and I have of you and your beloved brother will forever be etched in our hearts, souls, and minds.

At this writing, Michael and Quinnia are going their separate ways. It breaks our heart to see them split up. We only wish them both happiness as they move forward with their journeys.

Please note: Some of the names have been changed not so much to protect the innocent but rather the "not so innocent."

I did obtain permission from Tim Braun, Patrick Mathews, and Kirstin Ross to mention their real names during my readings with them. I encourage anybody reading this to seek them out, as they are the most wonderful and incredible mediums. I truly believe they have a gift from the Almighty and are put on earth to help us mortals who cannot see beyond that veil as they can.

I felt the need to share this poem that Brian wrote for his beloved, Simone. This definitely tells me that my son is in heaven and looking down upon us with love and tenderness. I believe he knows how much he is missed here on earth.

> *Endless love*
> *Our spiritual dove*
> *From heaven above*
> *Keep us safe down below*
> *Let us not melt fast but oh so slow*
> *Under a shady tree*
> *Our hearts melt with tender glee*
> *Just a perfect kiss between you and me.*

—Brian Dubrasky, 2017

The End

Acknowledgements

My heartfelt thanks to all those at Luminare Press who helped bring my book to fruition. It is my wish to thank each and every one of you for your expertise and your contribution to my story. From editing, cover design, and layout to my website, Kim, Jamie, Melissa, Jenny, and Patricia, you are the most awesome team! Thank you, thank you, thank you. Blessings to each and all!

If you are a parent who has lost a child and want to reach out feel free to contact me at janetdubrasky.com

If you liked my book and feel it helped you in some small way, please consider leaving a review on either Amazon or Goodreads.

www.ingramcontent.com/pod-product-compliance
Lightning Source LLC
LaVergne TN
LVHW021708060526
838200LV00050B/2564